Cycle
Tours

Surrey & West Sussex

Nick Cotton

Publisher: Cycle Tours is a joint venture between
CycleCity Guides and Cordee

CycleCity Guides
The Welsh Mill
Parkhill Drive
Frome
BA11 2LE
T: +44 (0)1373 453533

info@cyclecityguides.co.uk
www.cyclecityguides.co.uk

Cordee
11 Jacknell Road
Dodwells Bridge Industrial Estate
Hinckley
LE10 3BS
T: +44 (0)1455 611 185

charlie@cordee.co.uk
www.cordee.co.uk

ISBN: 978 1 904207 54 2

Ordnance
Survey

Printed by: Kingsdown
Picture credits: Nick Cotton

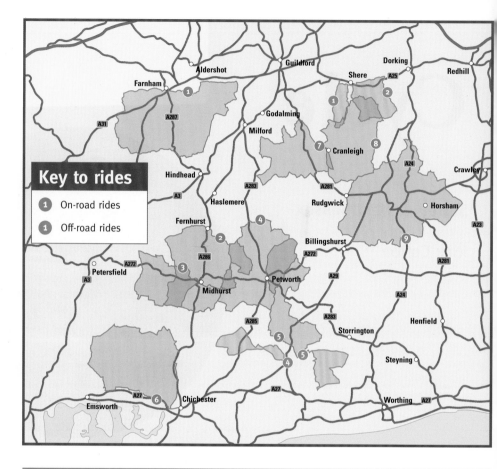

Key to rides

1 On-road rides

1 Off-road rides

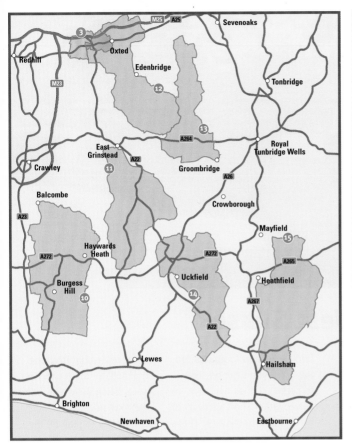

Grades

▲
Easy

▲▲
Easy / Moderate

▲▲▲
Moderate

▲▲▲▲
Moderate / Strenuous

▲▲▲▲▲
Strenuous

The grade is based on the amount of climbing involved and, for off-road routes, the roughness of the surface rather than the distance covered.

Key to rides

🔴 ① On-road rides

⚫ ① Off-road rides

Surrey & West Sussex

The geology of the area is dominated by three main features – the long chalk ridges of the North Downs and South Downs and, sandwiched between the two, the sandstone of the High Weald. The chalk downland offers the best mountain biking, especially along the top of the whaleback of hills running parallel with the South Coast that carries the South Downs Way from Winchester to Eastbourne. The South Downs Way has bridleway status along its entire length and makes a tough 2-3 day challenge.

By contrast the North Downs Way is a mixture of byways, bridleways and footpaths (on the latter you have no right to cycle) so rides here tend to link together short sections of byways and bridleways. These are rides that become more enjoyable with each outing as you come to recognise where the route goes without needing to refer to the map. Be warned that any ride on chalk and clay can get very muddy in the winter months or after heavy rain – these are definitely rides to enjoy after a few dry days in summer.

Surrey and West Sussex are two of the most densely populated counties in England and also some of the wealthiest, with high levels of car ownership resulting in almost all the A and B roads being busy with traffic. The road rides try as much as possible to stay on the network of quieter lanes, occasionally using railway paths such as the Cuckoo Trail, Worth Way, Forest Way or the Downs Link to avoid busy roads. With the same purpose in mind the odd stretch of bridleway or byway is used to offer direct crossings of A roads. Despite all this, you should be agreeably surprised by just how many miles of attractive quiet lanes still exist in the area.

Other useful information

Easy, traffic-free cycling for families and novices

Although the rides in this book are aimed at reasonably fit cyclists who are happy riding on the region's network of lanes or, in the case of mountain bikers, happy to ride on rough tracks, there may be times when your preference is for a ride that is also suitable for children or 'novice' cyclists. Listed below are some of the easier, flatter, traffic-free routes in the area.

West Sussex and Surrey have several traffic-free paths, in country parks, on dismantled railways converted to recreational use, along canal towpaths or in Forestry Commission holdings.

West Sussex

1. Worth Way
Railway path running for 6 miles west from East Grinstead to Worth on the east side of Crawley:
www.westsussex.gov.uk and search **'Worth Way'**

2. Centurion Way
Railway path running for 6 miles north from Chichester towards West Dean:
www.westsussex.gov.uk and search **'Centurion Way'**

3. Downs Link
A route linking the North Downs Way in Guildford to the South Downs Way in Shoreham, passing through Surrey and West Sussex, mainly along the course of an old railway line:
www.westsussex.gov.uk and search **'Downs Link'**

Surrey

1. Downs Link
See above

2. Wey Navigation
The best section for cycling lies to the south of Weybridge to Pyrford Lock (near Byfleet). Further south the towpath is a lot rougher. The most entertaining website about the area is:
www.weyriver.co.uk/theriver

3. Norbury Park, Leatherhead
Country park southeast of Leatherhead with a 4-mile waymarked circular ride:
www.mvcf.org.uk and click on **'Cycle Routes'** then **'Norbury Park'**
www.surreywildlifetrust.co.uk and click on **'Our Places'**

4. Horton Park, Epsom
Various traffic-free trails within this country park:
www.epsom-ewell.gov.uk and search **'Horton Park'**

5. Thames towpath, Weybridge to Putney Bridge
Follow the Thames from Weybridge into the heart of London:
www.sustrans.org.uk

6. Basingstoke Canal
Runs from Odiham in Hampshire to Byfleet (near Weybridge). The quality of the towpath varies:
www.basingstoke-canal.org.uk

Cycle shops in the area

See
www.isurrey.co.uk and search **'Cycle Shops'**
www.iwestsussex.co.uk and search **'Cycle Shops'**
www.thecyclepeople.com

Legend to 1:50,000 maps

Roads & paths

Motorway

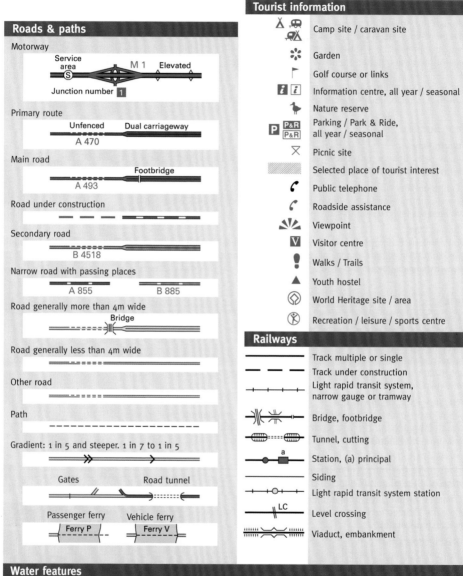

Service area (S) · Junction number 1 · M 1 · Elevated

Primary route

Unfenced · Dual carriageway · A 470

Main road

Footbridge · A 493

Road under construction

Secondary road

B 4518

Narrow road with passing places

A 855 · B 885

Road generally more than 4m wide

Bridge

Road generally less than 4m wide

Other road

Path

Gradient: 1 in 5 and steeper. 1 in 7 to 1 in 5

Gates · Road tunnel

Passenger ferry · Vehicle ferry

Ferry P · Ferry V

Tourist information

🏕 🚐	Camp site / caravan site
✳	Garden
⚑	Golf course or links
i **i**	Information centre, all year / seasonal
🦆	Nature reserve
P **P&R**	Parking / Park & Ride, all year / seasonal
✕	Picnic site
▨	Selected place of tourist interest
☎	Public telephone
☎	Roadside assistance
🔆	Viewpoint
V	Visitor centre
❗	Walks / Trails
▲	Youth hostel
◈	World Heritage site / area
⊗	Recreation / leisure / sports centre

Railways

———	Track multiple or single
– – –	Track under construction
┼┼┼	Light rapid transit system, narrow gauge or tramway
⇥⇤	Bridge, footbridge
◁▭▷	Tunnel, cutting
—●▪— a	Station, (a) principal
————	Siding
┼●┼	Light rapid transit system station
—— LC	Level crossing
▥▤▥	Viaduct, embankment

Water features

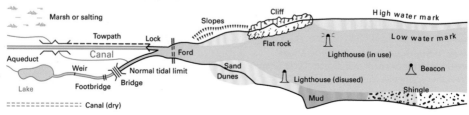

Marsh or salting · Towpath · Lock · Aqueduct · Canal · Weir · Footbridge · Bridge · Lake · Normal tidal limit · Ford · Canal (dry) · Slopes · Cliff · Flat rock · Sand · Dunes · Mud · High water mark · Low water mark · Lighthouse (in use) · Lighthouse (disused) · Beacon · Shingle

General features

⅏⅏⅏ ⅏⅏⅏	Cutting, embankment
(dotted)	Landfill site
(tree symbols)	Coniferous wood
(tree symbols)	Non-coniferous wood
(tree symbols)	Mixed wood
(symbols)	Orchard
(outline)	Park or ornamental ground
▣	Forestry Commission land
▣	National Trust - always open
▣	National Trust - limited access, observe local signs
▣	National Trust for Scotland - always open
▣	National Trust for Scotland - limited access, observe local signs
ʌ――ʌ――ʌ	Electricity transmission line (pylons shown at standard spacing)
> – –> – –>	Pipe line (arrow indicates direction of flow)
(symbol) ruin	Building
(symbol)	Important building (selected)
⬤	Bus or coach station
⬦	Glass structure
Ⓗ	Hospital
▮	Place of worship with tower
●	Place of worship with spire, dome or minaret
+	Place of worship
Ⴕ	Mast
ⵏ Ⴕ	Wind pump / wind turbine
ⵔ	Windmill with or without sails
+	Graticule intersection at 5' intervals

Rock features

Outcrop
Cliff
Scree
650
600

Public rights of way
(not applicable in Scotland)

··············	Footpath
–·–·–·–·–·	Restricted byway
– – – – –	Bridleway
–+–+–+–+–	Byway open to all traffic

Public rights of way shown have been taken from local authority definitive maps and later amendments. The symbols show the defined route so far as the scale of mapping will allow.

The representation on this map of any other road, track or path is no evidence of the existence of a right of way.

Other public access

· · · ·	Other route with public access
◆ ◆ ◆	National Trail, European Long Distance Path, Long Distance Route, selected Recreational Routes
● ● ●	On-road cycle route
○ ○ ○	Off-road cycle route
4	National Cycle Network Number
8	Regional Cycle Network Number
Danger Area	Firing and test ranges in the area Danger! Observe warning notices

Boundaries

+―+―+	National
–·–·–·–	District
–·–·–·–	County, region or island area
(shaded)	National Park

Abbreviations

CH	Clubhouse
PH	Public house
PC	Public convenience (in rural area)
TH	Town Hall, Guildhall or equivalent
CG	Cattle grid
P	Post office
MP	Milepost
MS	Mile stone

Antiquities

+	Position of antiquity that cannot be drawn to scale
☆ ····	Visible earthwork
VILLA	Roman
Castle	Non-Roman
✕	Battlefield (with date)

Heights

―50―	Contours are at 10 metre vertical intervals
·144	Heights are to the nearest metre above mean sea level
	Heights shown close to a triangulation pillar refer to the station height at ground level and not necessarily to the summit

Abbreviations and instructions

Instructions are given concisely to make them easy to follow while out riding. Remember to read one or two instructions ahead so that you do not miss a turning. This is most likely when you have to turn off a road / track you have been following for a while and are marked **Easy to miss** to warn you.

If there appears to be a contradiction between the instructions and what you actually see, always refer to the map. There are many reasons why, over the course of time, instructions may be subject to change with new roads, new junctions and new signposts.

Directions (all directions are given in bold)

L	left
R	right
SA	straight ahead
bear **L** or **R**	a turn which is less than 90 degrees (right-angle) at a fork in the road or on a sharp bend so that your course appears to be straight ahead; this is often written as 'in effect **SA**'
sharp **L** or **R**	a turn more acute than a right-angle
L or **R** sharply back on yourself	almost a U-turn
R then **L**	normally a T-junction where the next turn is visible from the first
R then first **L**	the second turning may be some distance from the first, ie '**R** then after ½ mile first **L**'

Junctions

T-j	T-junction, a junction where you have to give way
X-roads	crossroads, a junction where you may or may not have to give way
offset X-roads	the four roads are not in the form of a perfect cross and you will have to turn left then right, or vice versa, to continue the route

Signs

'Placename 2'	the words in quotation marks are those that appear on the signs, the numbers indicate the distance in miles unless stated otherwise
(NS)	not signposted

Instructions

An example of an easy instruction is:

4 At T-j at end of Smith Road by the White Swan Inn turn **R** on Brown Street 'Greentown 2, Redville 3'

There is more information in this instruction than you would normally need but things do change: pubs may close down and signs may be replaced, removed or vandalised.

An example of a difficult instruction is:

8 **Easy to miss:** shortly after the brow of the hill, on fast descent, first **R** (NS)

As you can see, there is no T-junction or 'Give Way' sign to halt you in your tracks, no signpost indicating where the right turn will take you and in addition you are picking up speed on a downhill, so you need to have your wits about you not to miss the turning.

Start

This is the suggested start point, coinciding with Instruction 1 on the map. There is no reason why you should not start at another point if it is more convenient.

Busy roads

These rides aim to keep to an absolute minimum time spent on busy roads but there are sometimes unavoidable sections where lane networks do not neatly link together. These busy roads are mentioned so that you are mentally prepared to deal with traffic, especially if there are children or less experienced cyclists in the group.

Off-road sections (on-road rides)

Occasionally a short distance on a traffic-free cyclepath, bridleway, byway or unclassified road can offer an alternative to a busy road. As the surfaces are not sealed you may encounter puddles or muddy water, especially in winter or after prolonged rain.

Terrain

This brief description of the terrain covered by the route should be read in conjunction with the cross-profile diagram at the foot of the page to help you plan your journey.

Distance

The distance (shown in miles and kilometres) is, of course, that from the beginning to the end of the ride. However, if you wish to shorten the ride because of tiredness, mechanical problems, a change in the weather or simply lack of time then the maps enable you to do so.

Grade

There are five grades of difficulty:
Easy
Easy / Moderate
Moderate
Moderate / Strenuous
Strenuous
The grade is based on the amount of climbing involved and, for off-road routes, the roughness of the surface rather than the distance covered.

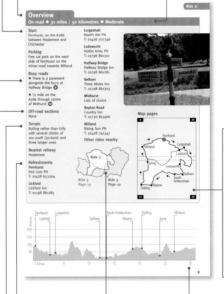

Map pages

Route overviews show how the maps have been laid out on the pages. Page numbers are shown in the corners. The diagrams show start points, route direction and some of the villages on or near the route.

Other rides nearby

Schematic map showing where nearby rides overlap. Shorter or longer rides can be created by mixing and matching rides.

Cross-profile

Shows heights in metres and distance travelled. Places along the route are shown.

Refreshments

More than three pubs or a mixture of pubs, cafés and tearooms in any one place is indicated by 'Lots of choice'. Otherwise, names of pubs, cafés and tearooms are listed, where possible with telephone numbers so that you can call ahead to check on opening times and when food is served.

Pines, heathland & quiet lanes south from Farnham

The ride starts from the bottom of Farnham's Castle Street, a wide, attractive street lined with Georgian houses leading up to the 12th century Norman castle. The first mile of the ride is unavoidably on busy streets as far as the railway station. Beyond here the ride takes you past the highly prosperous residences of Moor Park and parallel with the Hog's Back, a 500ft chalk ridge connecting Farnham to Guildford. Farnham is the starting point of the North Downs Way, a long-distance footpath also known as the Pilgrims Way which follows the ridge of chalk all the way to Canterbury and Dover. Eastwards to the pretty villages of Puttenham and Shackleford, with pines and bracken dominating on the sandy, well-drained soils of the Greensand Beds, spreading across the open heathland of the commons

of Crooksbury, Hankley and Ockley. After leaving the Elstead road near to Pitch Place you are plunged into a rollercoaster of tiny lanes as far as Churt. You soon cross into Hampshire and the landscape turns from heathland to arable farmland and becomes much less built-up in character. You may wish to stop at Binsted church to visit the grave of Viscount Montgomery

('Monty') of Alamein. Climb up to the ridge above Bentley then prepare yourself for more traffic for the final two miles (largely downhill) along Crondall Lane back into the heart of Farnham. There is a good traffic-free family ride in Alice Holt Forest, southwest of Farnham; similarly the largely improved towpath of the Basingstoke Canal can be followed from Odiham Castle to Woking.

Overview

On-road ● 35 miles / 56 kilometres ● Moderate

Start
Bottom of Castle Street, Farnham (west of Guildford)

Parking
Several Pay & Display car parks in Farnham

Busy roads
● The route through Farnham uses about 1 mile of busy streets ❶ to ❷

● About 3/4 mile on B3001 east of Elstead ⓬

● The final 2 miles down Crondall Lane back to the start can be busy ㉙

Off-road sections
None

Terrain
Undulating with a short, steep climb near the start through Moor Park, east of Farnham. Two longer climbs

Nearest railway
Farnham

Refreshments
Farnham
Lots of choice

The Sands
Barley Mow PH
T: 01252 782200

Puttenham
Good Intent PH
T: 01483 810387
Jolly Farmer PH
T: 01483 810374

Elstead
Woolpack PH
T: 01252 703106

Churt
Crossways PH
T: 01428 714323

Binsted
Cedars PH
T: 01420 22112

Bentley
Star Inn
T: 01420 23184

Other rides nearby
For rides just to the west of this one see *Cycle Tours – Hampshire & the Isle of Wight* by Nick Cotton

Map pages

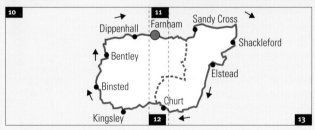

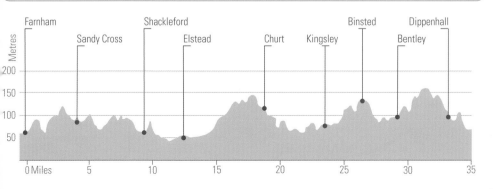

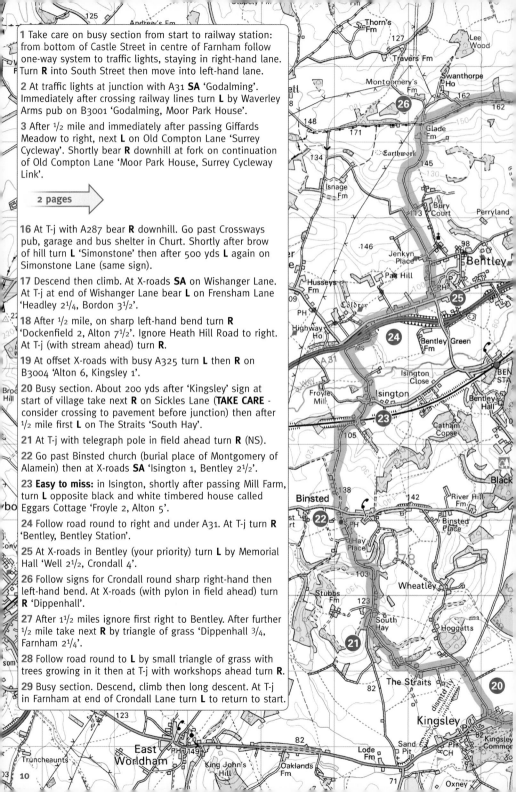

1 Take care on busy section from start to railway station: from bottom of Castle Street in centre of Farnham follow one-way system to traffic lights, staying in right-hand lane. Turn **R** into South Street then move into left-hand lane.

2 At traffic lights at junction with A31 **SA** 'Godalming'. Immediately after crossing railway lines turn **L** by Waverley Arms pub on B3001 'Godalming, Moor Park House'.

3 After ¹/₂ mile and immediately after passing Giffards Meadow to right, next **L** on Old Compton Lane 'Surrey Cycleway'. Shortly bear **R** downhill at fork on continuation of Old Compton Lane 'Moor Park House, Surrey Cycleway Link'.

2 pages ⟶

16 At T-j with A287 bear **R** downhill. Go past Crossways pub, garage and bus shelter in Churt. Shortly after brow of hill turn **L** 'Simonstone' then after 500 yds **L** again on Simonstone Lane (same sign).

17 Descend then climb. At X-roads **SA** on Wishanger Lane. At T-j at end of Wishanger Lane bear **L** on Frensham Lane 'Headley 2¹/₄, Bordon 3¹/₂'.

18 After ¹/₂ mile, on sharp left-hand bend turn **R** 'Dockenfield 2, Alton 7¹/₂'. Ignore Heath Hill Road to right. At T-j (with stream ahead) turn **R**.

19 At offset X-roads with busy A325 turn **L** then **R** on B3004 'Alton 6, Kingsley 1'.

20 Busy section. About 200 yds after 'Kingsley' sign at start of village take next **R** on Sickles Lane (**TAKE CARE** - consider crossing to pavement before junction) then after ¹/₂ mile first **L** on The Straits 'South Hay'.

21 At T-j with telegraph pole in field ahead turn **R** (NS).

22 Go past Binsted church (burial place of Montgomery of Alamein) then at X-roads **SA** 'Isington 1, Bentley 2¹/₂'.

23 Easy to miss: in Isington, shortly after passing Mill Farm, turn **L** opposite black and white timbered house called Eggars Cottage 'Froyle 2, Alton 5'.

24 Follow road round to right and under A31. At T-j turn **R** 'Bentley, Bentley Station'.

25 At X-roads in Bentley (your priority) turn **L** by Memorial Hall 'Well 2¹/₂, Crondall 4'.

26 Follow signs for Crondall round sharp right-hand then left-hand bend. At X-roads (with pylon in field ahead) turn **R** 'Dippenhall'.

27 After 1¹/₂ miles ignore first right to Bentley. After further ¹/₂ mile take next **R** by triangle of grass 'Dippenhall 3/4, Farnham 2¹/₄'.

28 Follow road round to **L** by small triangle of grass with trees growing in it then at T-j with workshops ahead turn **R**.

29 Busy section. Descend, climb then long descent. At T-j in Farnham at end of Crondall Lane turn **L** to return to start.

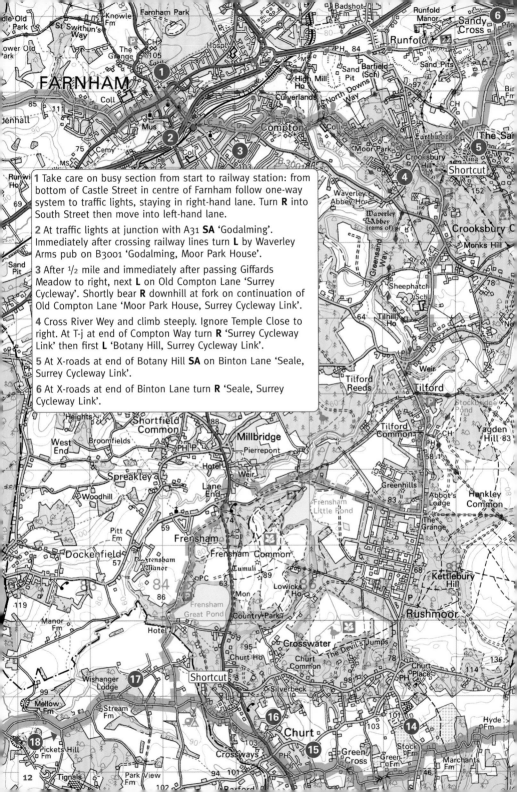

1 Take care on busy section from start to railway station: from bottom of Castle Street in centre of Farnham follow one-way system to traffic lights, staying in right-hand lane. Turn **R** into South Street then move into left-hand lane.

2 At traffic lights at junction with A31 **SA** 'Godalming'. Immediately after crossing railway lines turn **L** by Waverley Arms pub on B3001 'Godalming, Moor Park House'.

3 After 1/2 mile and immediately after passing Giffards Meadow to right, next **L** on Old Compton Lane 'Surrey Cycleway'. Shortly bear **R** downhill at fork on continuation of Old Compton Lane 'Moor Park House, Surrey Cycleway Link'.

4 Cross River Wey and climb steeply. Ignore Temple Close to right. At T-j at end of Compton Way turn **R** 'Surrey Cycleway Link' then first **L** 'Botany Hill, Surrey Cycleway Link'.

5 At X-roads at end of Botany Hill **SA** on Binton Lane 'Seale, Surrey Cycleway Link'.

6 At X-roads at end of Binton Lane turn **R** 'Seale, Surrey Cycleway Link'.

12

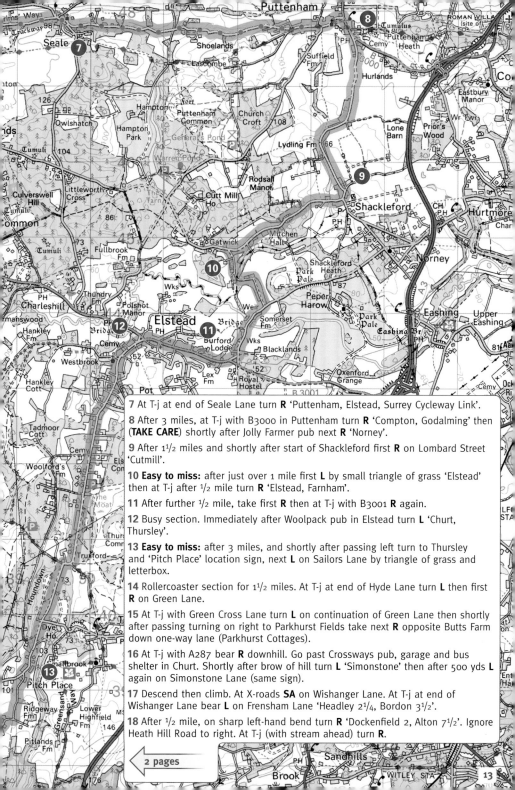

7 At T-j at end of Seale Lane turn **R** 'Puttenham, Elstead, Surrey Cycleway Link'.

8 After 3 miles, at T-j with B3000 in Puttenham turn **R** 'Compton, Godalming' then (**TAKE CARE**) shortly after Jolly Farmer pub next **R** 'Norney'.

9 After 1½ miles and shortly after start of Shackleford first **R** on Lombard Street 'Cutmill'.

10 Easy to miss: after just over 1 mile first **L** by small triangle of grass 'Elstead' then at T-j after ½ mile turn **R** 'Elstead, Farnham'.

11 After further ½ mile, take first **R** then at T-j with B3001 **R** again.

12 Busy section. Immediately after Woolpack pub in Elstead turn **L** 'Churt, Thursley'.

13 Easy to miss: after 3 miles, and shortly after passing left turn to Thursley and 'Pitch Place' location sign, next **L** on Sailors Lane by triangle of grass and letterbox.

14 Rollercoaster section for 1½ miles. At T-j at end of Hyde Lane turn **L** then first **R** on Green Lane.

15 At T-j with Green Cross Lane turn **L** on continuation of Green Lane then shortly after passing turning on right to Parkhurst Fields take next **R** opposite Butts Farm down one-way lane (Parkhurst Cottages).

16 At T-j with A287 bear **R** downhill. Go past Crossways pub, garage and bus shelter in Churt. Shortly after brow of hill turn **L** 'Simonstone' then after 500 yds **L** again on Simonstone Lane (same sign).

17 Descend then climb. At X-roads **SA** on Wishanger Lane. At T-j at end of Wishanger Lane bear **L** on Frensham Lane 'Headley 2¼, Bordon 3½'.

18 After ½ mile, on sharp left-hand bend turn **R** 'Dockenfield 2, Alton 7½'. Ignore Heath Hill Road to right. At T-j (with stream ahead) turn **R**.

← 2 pages

Fernhurst, Midhurst & the Rother Valley

ickfold, Lurgashall and Lodsworth sound like Sussex's answer to the 'Clunton and Clunbury, Clungunford and Clun' of A.E. Houseman's *Shropshire Lad*. They are three attractive villages set in the rolling Sussex woodland, each with a fine pub. After dropping down through Lickfold to the River Lod south of Lurgashall there is a long, steady climb alongside what must be one of the longest estate walls in the country, forming the boundary of Petwork Park. After a glimpse of the chalk whaleback of the South Downs ahead, more downs and ups follow, crossing the River Lod, climbing to Lurgashall then dropping again to the River Rother, the main watercourse running along the north side of the South Downs escarpment all the way from Petersfield to Pulborough. Quiet lanes take you to the edge of Midhurst, a handsome old market town with myriad cafés and pubs including the Spread Eagle, an impressive 15th century coaching inn. Each year the town hosts the Veuve Clicquot Gold Cup, a major polo competition. This is held on the Cowdray estate, with the final played outside the ruins of Cowdray Castle. Soon after leaving Midhurst you return to the lane network running along the base of the South Downs. Turning north at Didling, the route recrosses the River Rother, climbs through thick woodland and passes between a dramatic stone cutting at the top of Dunner Hill. Milland is your last chance of refreshment before the gentle climb back up to Fernhurst.

Overview
On-road ● 31 miles / 50 kilometres ● Moderate

Start
Fernhurst, on the A286
between Haslemere and
Chichester

Parking
Free car park on the west
side of Fernhurst on the
minor road towards Milland

Busy roads
● There is a pavement
alongside the A272 at
Halfway Bridge ⑧

● ½ mile on the
A286 through centre
of Midhurst ⑫

Off-road sections
None

Terrain
Rolling rather than hilly
with several climbs of
100-200ft (30-60m) and
three longer ones

Nearest railway
Haslemere

Refreshments
Fernhurst
Red Lion PH
T: 01428 653304

Lickfold
Lickfold Inn
T: 01798 861285

Lurgashall
Noah's Ark PH
T: 01428 707346

Lodsworth
Hollist Arms PH
T: 01798 861310

Halfway Bridge
Halfway Bridge Inn
T: 01798 861281

Selham
Three Moles Inn
T: 01798 861303

Midhurst
Lots of choice

Bepton Road
Country Inn
T: 01730 813466

Milland
Rising Sun PH
T: 01428 741347

Other rides nearby

Ride 2

Ride 3
Page 20

Ride 4
Page 26

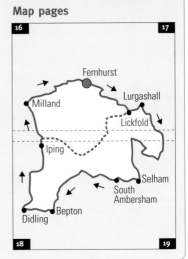

Map pages

16   17

Fernhurst

Milland

Lurgashall

Lickfold

Iping

Selham

South
Ambersham

Bepton

Didling

18   19

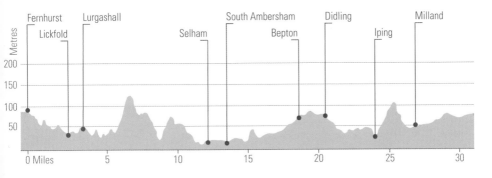

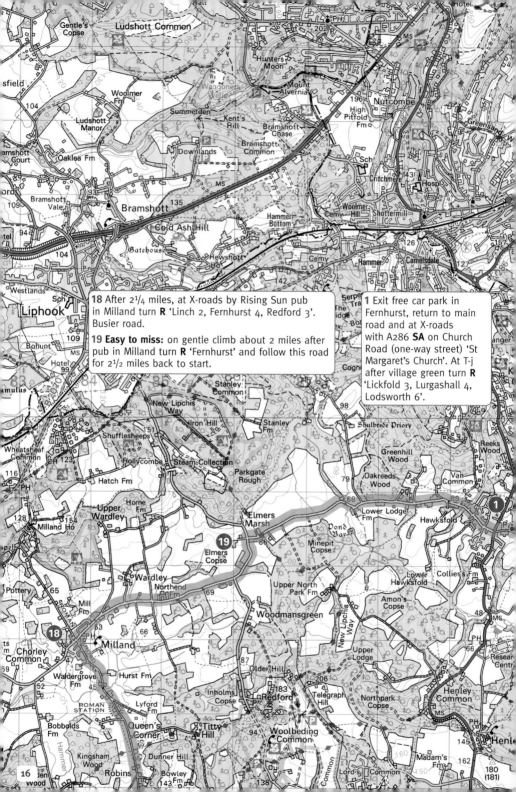

18 After 2¼ miles, at X-roads by Rising Sun pub in Milland turn **R** 'Linch 2, Fernhurst 4, Redford 3'. Busier road.

19 Easy to miss: on gentle climb about 2 miles after pub in Milland turn **R** 'Fernhurst' and follow this road for 2½ miles back to start.

1 Exit free car park in Fernhurst, return to main road and at X-roads with A286 **SA** on Church Road (one-way street) 'St Margaret's Church'. At T-j after village green turn **R** 'Lickfold 3, Lurgashall 4, Lodsworth 6'.

2 After 2½ miles, at T-j by Lickfold Inn turn **L** 'Haslemere 6, Lurgashall 1' then shortly first **R** 'Lurgashall'.

3 After 1 mile, and just before village green and telephone box in Lurgashall turn **R** sharply back on yourself (NS).

4 At T-j after a further mile, with stone wall ahead turn **R** (NS).

2 pages →

11 After 2¼ miles at T-j at end of Selham Road turn **R** 'Midhurst' then immediately after Spread Eagle pub and before Swan Inn next **L** on West Street.

12 At mini-roundabout turn **L** on busy A286 towards Cocking and Singleton. After ½ mile, on left-hand bend turn **R** 'Bepton'.

13 Go past Country Inn then at T-j almost 2 miles after pub, turn **R** 'Didling 2, Harting 6, Parish Church'.

14 After 1½ miles at 2-way signpost in triangle of grass turn **R** 'Ingrams Green'.

15 At T-j after 2 miles turn **R** 'Iping, Midhurst'.

16 Busier road. After 1¼ miles at offset X-roads with A272 turn **R** then **L** 'Iping ½, Milland 3'.

17 At X-roads **SA** (your priority) 'Liphook 5, Milland 2'. Climb then descend.

2 pages

18

Ride 4 also goes through Lodsworth. Page 26

Ride 3 also goes through South Ambersham. Page 20

5 After 2 miles, ignore right turn to River Common (no through road) and keep following massive long wall to left. Climb to top of hill then take first **R** 'Pitshill'.

6 Very easy to miss: after ½ mile of fast descent (keep your brakes on!) turn first **R** (NS), immediately after first house on right.

7 Long descent to cross river. Climb for almost 1 mile then at T-j bear **L** 'Lodsworth'.

8 Go through Lodsworth and past Hollist Arms pub. At T-j with busy A272 turn **L** along pavement then **R** opposite Halfway Bridge Inn 'Graffham 3, Selham 1, South Ambersham 2'.

9 Cross River Rother then first **R** 'South Ambersham, Midhurst'.

10 Go past polo ground to your left. At T-j turn **R** 'Midhurst' then shortly **L** 'West Lavington, Midhurst'.

West from Midhurst along the foot of the South Downs

The prosperous town of Midhurst is a good base for rides to the east and west along the valley of the River Rother, running along the base of the South Downs. This ride does a bit of both, heading east from Midhurst before crossing the A286 at Cocking and exploring lanes further west. Devising cycle rides in the built-up South East of England is often a case of joining the dots, the dots being the safe crossings of busy A roads. The minor lane crossing of the A286 at Cocking is one of the few that exist on this

road between Midhurst all the way south to Chichester, and offers a good excuse to take a meandering course along the delightful lanes through South Ambersham and Heyshott, with an even more minor one linking Heyshott to Cocking. The South Downs are constant companions on this trip along the base of the escarpment. The South Downs stretch for about 70 miles from west to east and are the southern remnant of the Wealden dome, laid down 60 million years ago as a shallow sea. The rock consists of the

microscopic skeletons of plankton which lived in the sea, hence the white colour of the chalk. Erosion has removed the central part of the chalk dome revealing the harder rocks of the High Weald beneath it. Back on the ride, turn north in East Harting, cross the A272 at Rogate and climb through woodland to the ridge. If there were quiet, little-used lanes on the outward trip, then the lanes east from Chithurst towards Woolbeding are extraordinary.

Overview
On-road ● 23 miles / 47 kilometres ● Moderate

Start & Parking
North Street car park at the north end of Midhurst, on the A286 between Haslemere and Chichester

Busy roads
400yds on the A272 on the return to Midhurst **20**

Off-road sections
None, although the lane east from Chithurst is almost a track

Terrain
Undulating with several climbs of 100-200ft (30-60m) and one longer one

Nearest railway
Liss

Refreshments
Midhurst
Lots of choice

Heyshott
Unicorn Inn
T: 01730 813486

Cocking
Blue Bell PH
T: 01730 813449

Elsted
Three Horseshoes PH
T: 01730 825746

Rogate
White Horse Inn
T: 01730 821333

Map pages

Other rides nearby
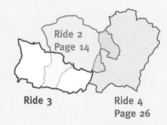

Ride 2
Page 14

Ride 3

Ride 4
Page 26

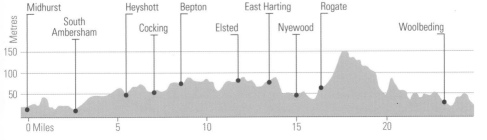

11 At next T-j by 3-way signpost and triangle of grass turn **R** 'Liphook 8, Rogate 2, Nyewood'.

12 Busier road. After 2 miles, at X-roads with A272 by White Horse Inn in Rogate, **SA** 'Rake 2½, Liss 3½'.

13 Climb for 1 mile up through woodland. At X-roads at top (your priority) turn **R** 'Chithurst 3½'.

14 After 1½ miles at T-j by triangle of grass turn sharp **L** 'Borden Wood, Milland'.

15 Descend, following road round very sharp right-hand bend. At T-j turn **R** 'Chithurst 1'.

16 Climb. **Easy to miss:** on descent, pass under power lines then shortly, on sharp right-hand bend, turn **L** gently uphill (NS).

17 Descend to cross stream. At T-j by triangle of grass turn **L** then **R** uphill 'Hammerwood'.

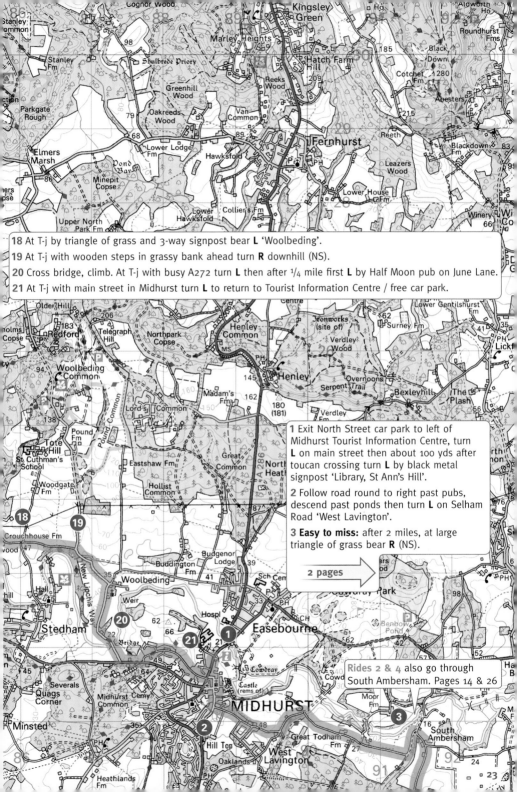

18 At T-j by triangle of grass and 3-way signpost bear **L** 'Woolbeding'.

19 At T-j with wooden steps in grassy bank ahead turn **R** downhill (NS).

20 Cross bridge, climb. At T-j with busy A272 turn **L** then after ¼ mile first **L** by Half Moon pub on June Lane.

21 At T-j with main street in Midhurst turn **L** to return to Tourist Information Centre / free car park.

1 Exit North Street car park to left of Midhurst Tourist Information Centre, turn **L** on main street then about 100 yds after toucan crossing turn **L** by black metal signpost 'Library, St Ann's Hill'.

2 Follow road round to right past pubs, descend past ponds then turn **L** on Selham Road 'West Lavington'.

3 Easy to miss: after 2 miles, at large triangle of grass bear **R** (NS).

2 pages

Rides 2 & 4 also go through South Ambersham. Pages 14 & 26

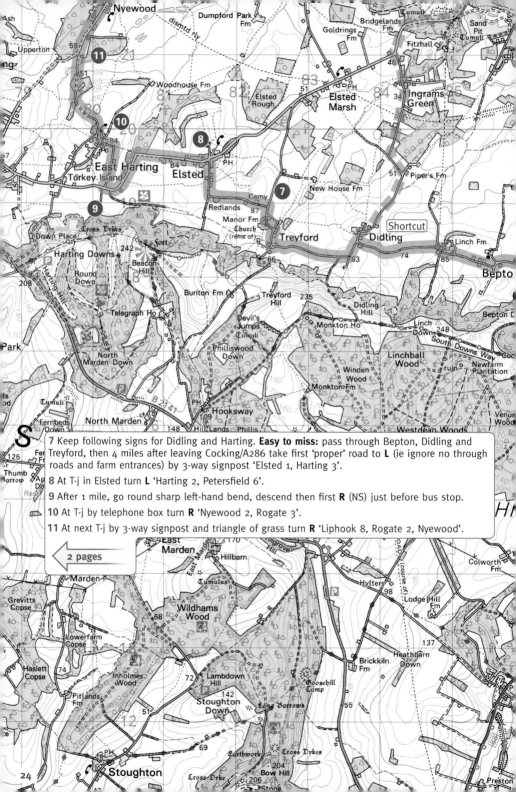

7 Keep following signs for Didling and Harting. **Easy to miss:** pass through Bepton, Didling and Treyford, then 4 miles after leaving Cocking/A286 take first 'proper' road to **L** (ie ignore no through roads and farm entrances) by 3-way signpost 'Elsted 1, Harting 3'.

8 At T-j in Elsted turn **L** 'Harting 2, Petersfield 6'.

9 After 1 mile, go round sharp left-hand bend, descend then first **R** (NS) just before bus stop.

10 At T-j by telephone box turn **R** 'Nyewood 2, Rogate 3'.

11 At next T-j by 3-way signpost and triangle of grass turn **R** 'Liphook 8, Rogate 2, Nyewood'.

← 2 pages

24

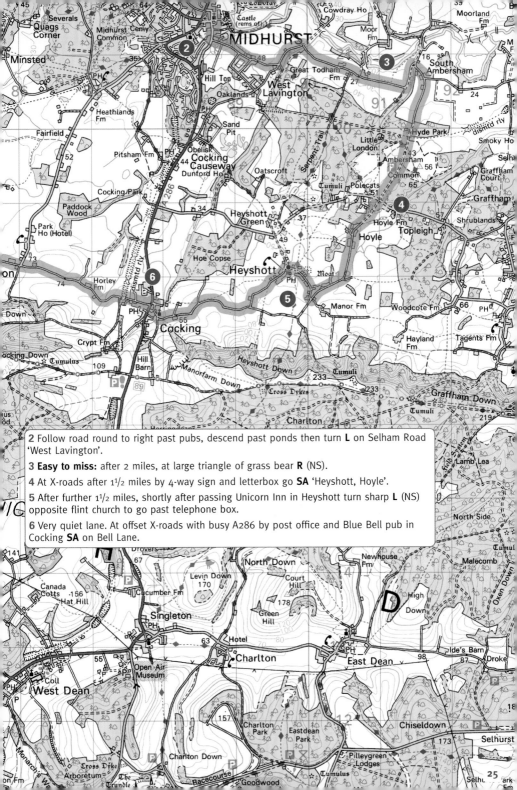

2 Follow road round to right past pubs, descend past ponds then turn **L** on Selham Road 'West Lavington'.

3 Easy to miss: after 2 miles, at large triangle of grass bear **R** (NS).

4 At X-roads after 1½ miles by 4-way sign and letterbox go **SA** 'Heyshott, Hoyle'.

5 After further 1½ miles, shortly after passing Unicorn Inn in Heyshott turn sharp **L** (NS) opposite flint church to go past telephone box.

6 Very quiet lane. At offset X-roads with busy A286 by post office and Blue Bell pub in Cocking **SA** on Bell Lane.

25

North of Petworth on woodland lanes & woodland tracks

There are a couple of short sections of track used on this ride which will either be the most memorable part of your day out or will be a reason for you to take pins to an effigy of the author. These tracks are best avoided on lightweight bikes with narrow tyres or in the depths of winter. The tracks are used to avoid spending time on the busy roads that make route-finding around the handsome town of Petworth something of a challenge. Petworth House was built in the 17th century by the Duke of Somerset and its landscaped estate inspired the painter Turner, who had a studio there. The ride leaves and returns to Petworth on what is the best and quietest exit from the town – south on Grove Lane. A pavement alongside the A285 is a convenient link between the lane networks to the west and east of this main road. After crossing the River Rother near to South Ambersham you arrive at the busy A272 and may wonder where to go – the answer is to dive into the woodland ahead on a narrow sunken track that neatly avoids the traffic and joins a delightful minor lane after 350 yards. Lodsworth, Lickfold and Lurgashall sounds like some sort of tongue-twister, but these are pretty Sussex villages each with a fine pub that take you north towards Northchapel. Tiny lanes lead through Kirdford, across the A272 and on to the second, longer track by the Welldiggers pub, this time avoiding the A283 and soon rejoining the outward route.

Overview
On-road ● 28 miles / 45 kilometres ● Moderate

Start
The main square in Petworth, at junction of A272 and A283 to the north of Bognor Regis

Parking
Several Pay & Display car parks in Petworth

Busy roads
● The 'minor' road linking the A285 and the A283 just south of Petworth **2**

● A285 at Heath End (use pavement) **4**

● A286 in Northchapel **14**

Off-road sections
● About 350yds on narrow stone track north of the A272 between South Ambersham and Lodsworth **8**

● About 600yds on broad stone-based track south of the A283 near Byworth towards the end of the ride **20**

Terrain
Undulating with several climbs of 100-200ft (30-60m) and three longer climbs

Nearest railway
Pulborough

Refreshments
Petworth
Lots of choice

Graffham
Foresters Arms PH
Tel: 01798 867202
White Horse PH
T: 01798 867331

Lodsworth
Hollist Arms PH
T: 01798 861281

Lickfold
Lickfold Inn
T: 01798 861285

Lurgashall
Noah's Ark Inn
T: 01428 707346

Northchapel
Half Moon Inn
T: 01428 707270

Kirdford
Foresters Arms PH
T: 01403 820205

Byworth
Welldiggers PH
T: 01798 342287

Other rides nearby
Ride 2
Page 14

Ride 3
Page 20

Ride 4

Ride 5
Page 32

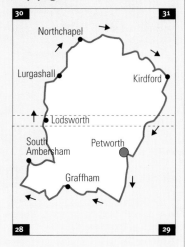

Map pages

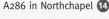

30   31

Northchapel

Lurgashall   Kirdford

Lodsworth

South Ambersham   Petworth

Graffham

28   29

Petworth   South Ambersham   Lurgashall

Graffham   Lodsworth   Northchapel   Kirdford

Kirdford

Metres

150

100

50

0 Miles   5   10   15   20   25

Rides 2 & 3 also pass through South Ambersham. Pages 14 & 20

4 At T-j with busy A285 turn **L** 'Duncton 1, Chichester 12'. Use 'cyclepath' in verge then take first **R** 'Selham 3, Graffham 3'.

5 At X-roads (your priority) after 1¹/₂ miles turn **L** 'Graffham'.

6 After 1¹/₄ miles, in Graffham, with 'No through road' sign ahead turn **R** 'Heyshott, Midhurst, Cocking'.

7 Follow road round sharp right-hand then left-hand bend, ignoring turns. At X-roads by 4-way signpost and letterbox turn **R** 'Ambersham'.

8 After 1¹/₂ miles, ignore right turn then left turn by large triangle of grass. Cross River Rother then at T-j with busy A272 go **SA** on track in woods opposite 'Public Right of Way'. Push your bike on this narrow woodland path for 350 yds, however improbable it may seem.

9 At T-j with lane bear **R** then shortly, at next T-j bear **L** downhill (NS). At fork of roads after ¹/₂ mile by 'Lodsworth' village sign and triangle of grass bear **L** on Heath End Lane and shortly **L** again on School Lane.

10 At T-j at end of School Lane bear **L** on Smithbrook. Follow signs for Haslemere and Lurgashall.

2 pages ⟹

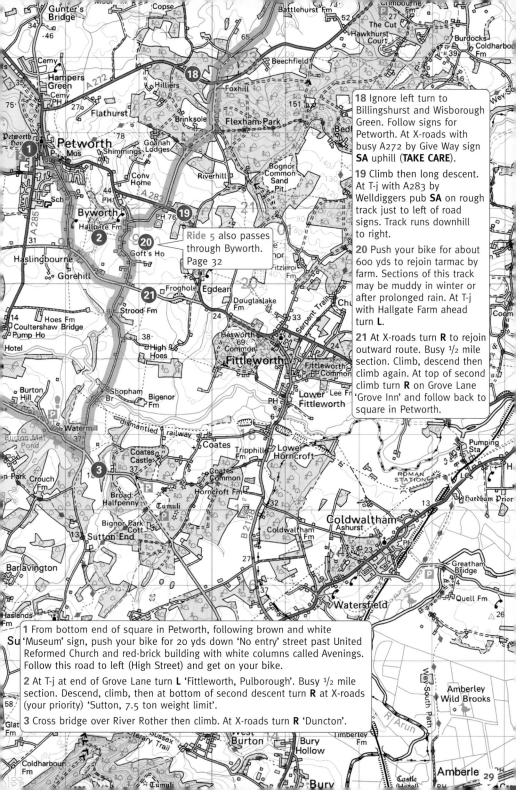

18 Ignore left turn to Billingshurst and Wisborough Green. Follow signs for Petworth. At X-roads with busy A272 by Give Way sign **SA** uphill (**TAKE CARE**).

19 Climb then long descent. At T-j with A283 by Welldiggers pub **SA** on rough track just to left of road signs. Track runs downhill to right.

20 Push your bike for about 600 yds to rejoin tarmac by farm. Sections of this track may be muddy in winter or after prolonged rain. At T-j with Hallgate Farm ahead turn **L**.

21 At X-roads turn **R** to rejoin outward route. Busy ½ mile section. Climb, descend then climb again. At top of second climb turn **R** on Grove Lane 'Grove Inn' and follow back to square in Petworth.

Ride 5 also passes through Byworth. Page 32

1 From bottom end of square in Petworth, following brown and white 'Museum' sign, push your bike for 20 yds down 'No entry' street past United Reformed Church and red-brick building with white columns called Avenings. Follow this road to left (High Street) and get on your bike.

2 At T-j at end of Grove Lane turn **L** 'Fittleworth, Pulborough'. Busy ½ mile section. Descend, climb, then at bottom of second descent turn **R** at X-roads (your priority) 'Sutton, 7.5 ton weight limit'.

3 Cross bridge over River Rother then climb. At X-roads turn **R** 'Duncton'.

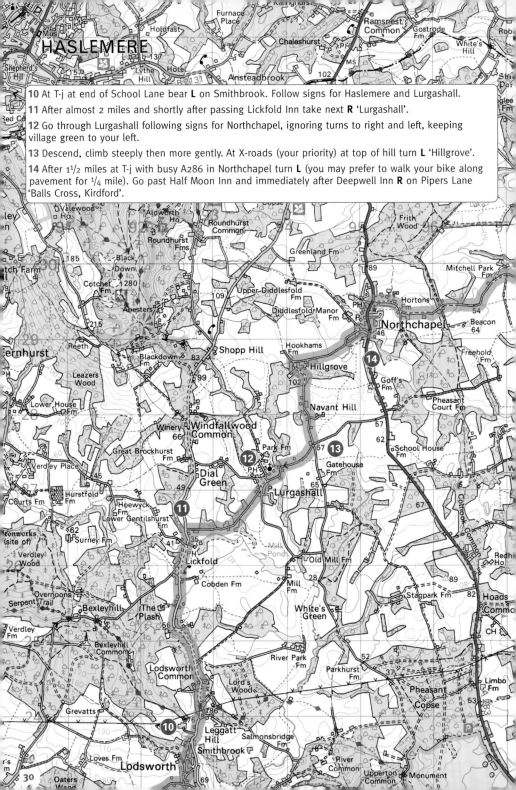

10 At T-j at end of School Lane bear **L** on Smithbrook. Follow signs for Haslemere and Lurgashall.

11 After almost 2 miles and shortly after passing Lickfold Inn take next **R** 'Lurgashall'.

12 Go through Lurgashall following signs for Northchapel, ignoring turns to right and left, keeping village green to your left.

13 Descend, climb steeply then more gently. At X-roads (your priority) at top of hill turn **L** 'Hillgrove'.

14 After 1½ miles at T-j with busy A286 in Northchapel turn **L** (you may prefer to walk your bike along pavement for ¼ mile). Go past Half Moon Inn and immediately after Deepwell Inn **R** on Pipers Lane 'Balls Cross, Kirdford'.

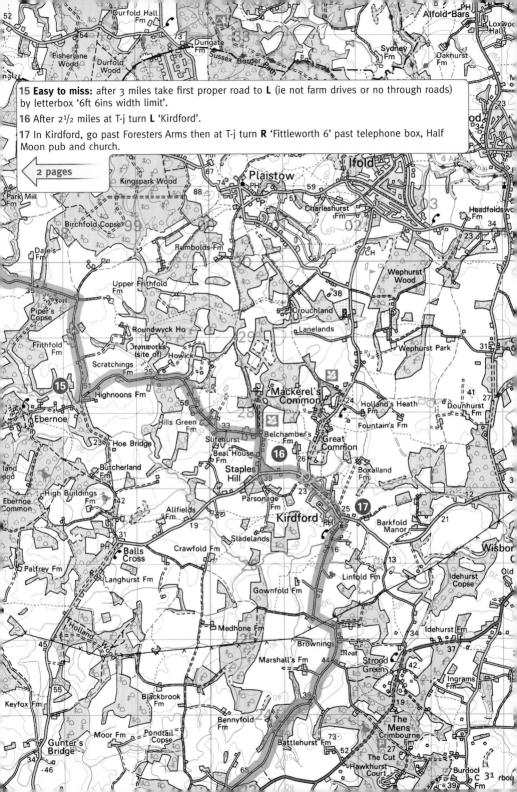

15 Easy to miss: after 3 miles take first proper road to **L** (ie not farm drives or no through roads) by letterbox '6ft 6ins width limit'.

16 After 2½ miles at T-j turn **L** 'Kirdford'.

17 In Kirdford, go past Foresters Arms then at T-j turn **R** 'Fittleworth 6' past telephone box, Half Moon pub and church.

2 pages

Petworth, the Roman villa at Bignor & Amberley

P etworth is one of those very attractive towns that is dominated by the busy roads that run through it and past it. For cyclists there is one good exit to the south that avoids almost all the traffic, soon dropping to cross the River Rother then climbing to the

pretty villages of Sutton and Bignor, the latter famous for its Roman Villa, which you pass on the course of the ride. The villa had 65 rooms with superb mosaics and the Roman road known as Stane Street, connecting Chichester to London, runs nearby. Views of the South Downs

dominate the first half of the ride. From Bignor you drop down almost to sea level at the crossing of the River Arun near Amberley station. The B2139 is a fast and busy road and you are advised to use the tarmac path alongside the road (with consideration for other users). Amberley itself is much quieter and full of fine houses and a castle, now an upmarket hotel. Avoiding main roads means braving one short (400yds) stretch of track beyond Fittleworth. This enables you to cross the A283 almost directly from one lane network to the next. To the north of the A283 you follow a wooded lane so quiet that you may struggle to believe you are in the built-up South East of England. Be warned that from crossing the A283 you should not attempt any shortcut back to Petworth as this will commit you to the busy and dangerous A272.

Overview
On-road ● **31 miles / 50 kilometres** ● **Moderate**

Start
Main square in Petworth

Parking
Several Pay & Display car parks in Petworth

Busy roads
● 1¹/₂ miles on the B2139 through Amberley Station **7** to **8**

● ³/₄ mile on the A283 / A272 back into Petworth (30mph speed limit) **23**

Off-road sections
400yds of track west of the Swan Inn in Fittleworth (stone-based but may be muddy after rain) **15**

Terrain
Generally undulating in the valleys formed by the River Rother and the River Arun. One longer 415ft (126m) climb from crossing the River Rother up into the wooded hills north of Fittleworth **14** to **19**

Nearest railway
Amberley

Refreshments
Petworth
Lots of choice

Sutton
White Horse Inn
T: 01798 869221

Bury
Squire & Horse Inn
T: 01798 831343

Houghton
George & Dragon PH
T: 01798 831559

Amberley village
Black Horse PH
T: 01798 831552
Sportsman PH
T: 01798 831787

Fittleworth
Swan Inn
T: 01798 865429

Kirdford
Half Moon PH
T: 01403 820223

Balls Cross
Stag Inn
T: 01403 820241

Other rides nearby

Ride 5

Ride 4
Page 26

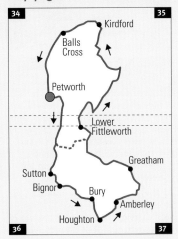

Map pages

34   35
Kirdford
Balls Cross
Petworth
Lower Fittleworth
Greatham
Sutton
Bignor   Bury
Houghton   Amberley
36   37

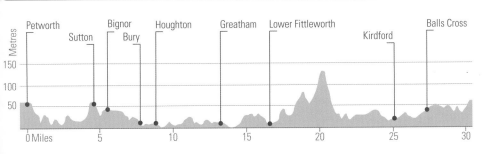

Petworth   Bignor   Houghton   Greatham   Lower Fittleworth   Balls Cross

Sutton   Bury   Kirdford

Metres

150
100
50

0 Miles   5   10   15   20   25   30

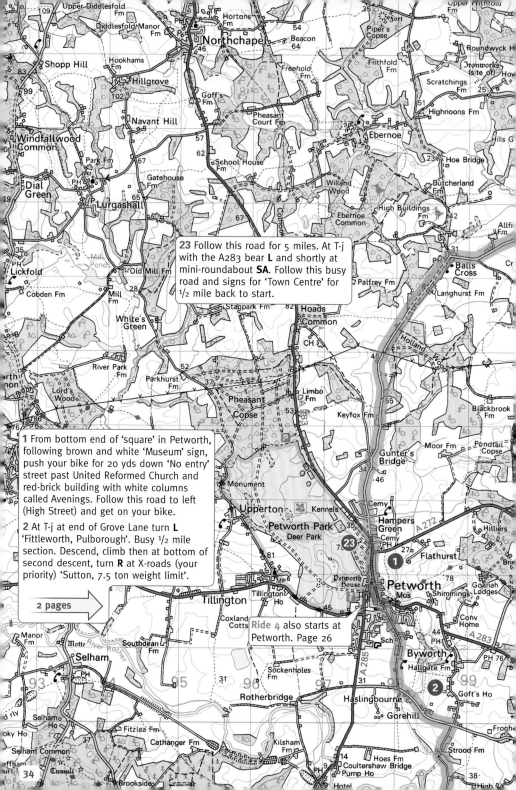

23 Follow this road for 5 miles. At T-j with the A283 bear **L** and shortly at mini-roundabout **SA**. Follow this busy road and signs for 'Town Centre' for ½ mile back to start.

1 From bottom end of 'square' in Petworth, following brown and white 'Museum' sign, push your bike for 20 yds down 'No entry' street past United Reformed Church and red-brick building with white columns called Avenings. Follow this road to left (High Street) and get on your bike.

2 At T-j at end of Grove Lane turn **L** 'Fittleworth, Pulborough'. Busy ½ mile section. Descend, climb then at bottom of second descent, turn **R** at X-roads (your priority) 'Sutton, 7.5 ton weight limit'.

2 pages ➡

Ride 4 also starts at Petworth. Page 26

16 At T-j with A283 turn **L** then **R**.

17 After 1 mile at fork bear **R** then at T-j **R** again (NS).

18 Shortly at next fork bear **L** on upper lane then at T-j turn **L** 'Single track road'.

19 Climb, descend through steep cutting, ignoring left turn to Bedham and Petworth. Follow signs for Wisborough Green. Ignore another left turn on Brick Kiln Common. Descend past black wooden barns and take next **L** 'Kirdford 3'.

20 At X-roads with A272 **SA** '6ft 6ins width limit'.

21 At T-j by triangle of grass with letterbox in brick pillar turn **R** 'Kirdford, Plaistow'.

22 Immediately after Half Moon pub in Kirdford, next **L** 'Petworth'.

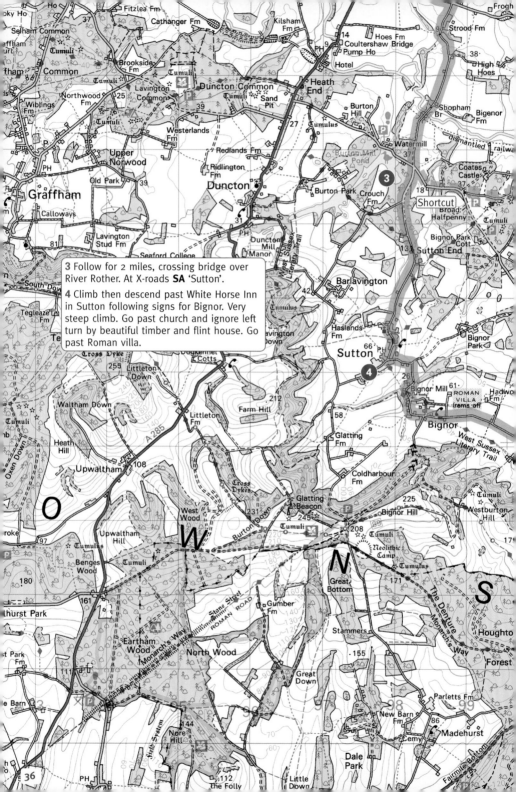

3 Follow for 2 miles, crossing bridge over River Rother. At X-roads **SA** 'Sutton'.

4 Climb then descend past White Horse Inn in Sutton following signs for Bignor. Very steep climb. Go past church and ignore left turn by beautiful timber and flint house. Go past Roman villa.

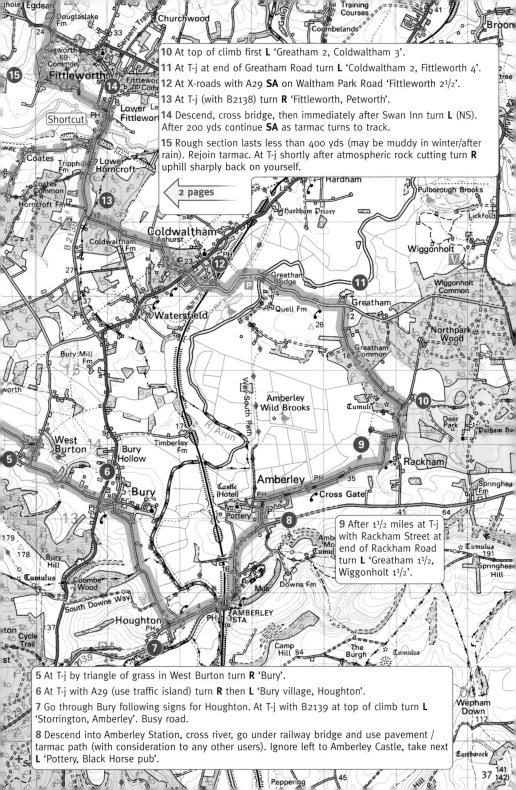

10 At top of climb first **L** 'Greatham 2, Coldwaltham 3'.

11 At T-j at end of Greatham Road turn **L** 'Coldwaltham 2, Fittleworth 4'.

12 At X-roads with A29 **SA** on Waltham Park Road 'Fittleworth 2½'.

13 At T-j (with B2138) turn **R** 'Fittleworth, Petworth'.

14 Descend, cross bridge, then immediately after Swan Inn turn **L** (NS). After 200 yds continue **SA** as tarmac turns to track.

15 Rough section lasts less than 400 yds (may be muddy in winter/after rain). Rejoin tarmac. At T-j shortly after atmospheric rock cutting turn **R** uphill sharply back on yourself.

← 2 pages

9 After 1½ miles at T-j with Rackham Street at end of Rackham Road turn **L** 'Greatham 1½, Wiggonholt 1½'.

5 At T-j by triangle of grass in West Burton turn **R** 'Bury'.

6 At T-j with A29 (use traffic island) turn **R** then **L** 'Bury village, Houghton'.

7 Go through Bury following signs for Houghton. At T-j with B2139 at top of climb turn **L** 'Storrington, Amberley'. Busy road.

8 Descend into Amberley Station, cross river, go under railway bridge and use pavement / tarmac path (with consideration to any other users). Ignore left to Amberley Castle, take next **L** 'Pottery, Black Horse pub'.

Chichester & the South Downs

S tarting from the heart of the attractive city of Chichester with its famous Norman cathedral, this ride is an exploration of the rolling countryside lying inland from the coast with the added bonus of a flat traffic-free return into the heart of the city. Chichester's history goes back to Roman times as testified by the four-quarter layout and the city walls. The Market Cross dates from the 15th century and there are many fine Georgian houses throughout the city. If you are interested in Roman history you may wish to divert off the route just west of the start to visit Fishbourne, a sumptuous Roman palace with magnificent mosaics, the largest Roman building found in Britain, discovered in 1960 by workmen laying a water pipe. The ride falls easily into three parts: the first runs west from Chichester to Rowlands Castle, largely along the course of the waymarked South Coast Cycle Route, the best option to avoid the A27 and the A259; the second

part takes you north then east through rolling downland on tiny, quiet lanes between Finchdean and West Dean; the final part is traffic-free south from West Dean on a vergeside path then the Centurion Way, a converted railway path. There are some wonderful metal sculptures of Roman soldiers representing

the work gang that originally built the roads. Another option for a cycle ride from Chichester is to follow the waymarked Salterns Way around the harbour to West Itchenor. For more details go to www.conservancy.co.uk, click on 'Out & About' then 'Cycling'.

Overview
On-road ● 31 miles / 50 kilometres ● Easy / Moderate

Start
Chichester Cathedral
(alternative starting options
are Rowlands Castle or
West Dean)

Parking
Lots of Pay & Display car
parks in Chichester

Busy roads
Many of the 'minor' roads
between Chichester and
Rowlands Castle are busier
than one might expect. The
busy 3/4 mile section on
the B2141 near Chilgrove is
downhill and quickly over 18

Off-road sections
Roadside pavement / cyclepath
south from West Dean then
smooth stone-based Centurion
Way back to Chichester. One
short rough section linking the
two 23 to 25

Terrain
Generally flat in the southern
half of the ride. Rolling
downland in northern half
with four climbs of about 200ft
(60m)

Nearest railway
Chichester or Rowlands Castle

Refreshments
Chichester
Lots of choice

Woodmancote
Woodmancote Arms PH
T: 01243 372612

Westbourne
Lots of choice

Rowlands Castle
Lots of choice, including
café near railway arches

Finchdean
George PH
T: 02392 412257

West Dean
Selsey Arms PH
T: 01243 811465

Other rides nearby
Although Rides 2 and 3 are
both close by there are no
safe roads easily connecting
this ride to them. It would
be better to do this ride then
drive to Midhurst to do the
others. For rides just to the
west of this one see *Cycle
Tours – Hampshire & the Isle
of Wight* by Nick Cotton

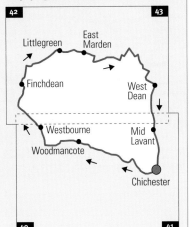

Map pages

42		43
	East	
Littlegreen	Marden	
Finchdean		West Dean
	Westbourne	Mid
		Lavant
Woodmancote		
		Chichester
40		41

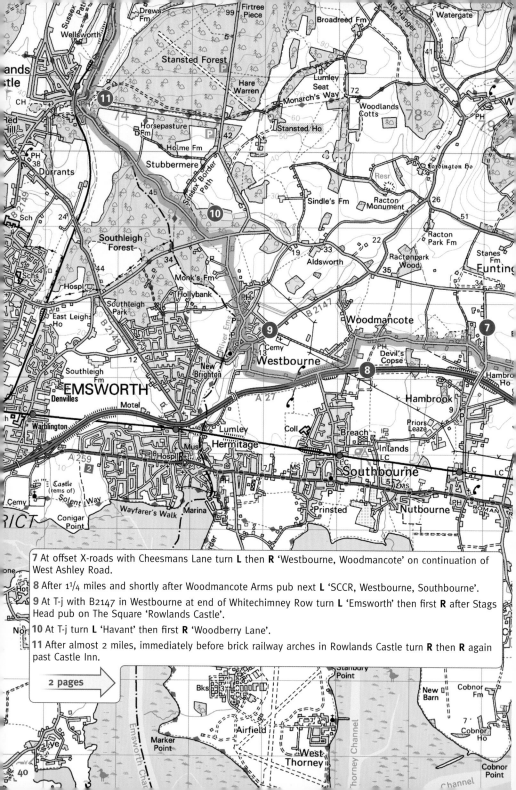

7 At offset X-roads with Cheesmans Lane turn **L** then **R** 'Westbourne, Woodmancote' on continuation of West Ashley Road.

8 After 1¼ miles and shortly after Woodmancote Arms pub next **L** 'SCCR, Westbourne, Southbourne'.

9 At T-j with B2147 in Westbourne at end of Whitechimney Row turn **L** 'Emsworth' then first **R** after Stags Head pub on The Square 'Rowlands Castle'.

10 At T-j turn **L** 'Havant' then first **R** 'Woodberry Lane'.

11 After almost 2 miles, immediately before brick railway arches in Rowlands Castle turn **R** then **R** again past Castle Inn.

2 pages

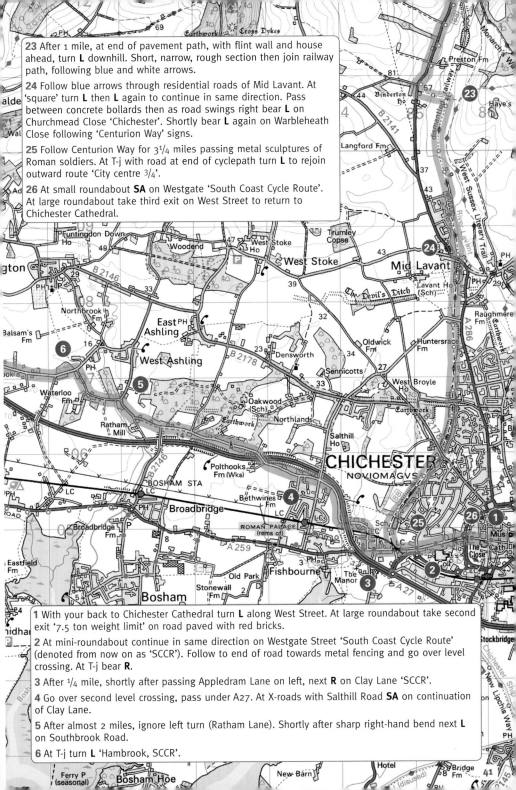

23 After 1 mile, at end of pavement path, with flint wall and house ahead, turn **L** downhill. Short, narrow, rough section then join railway path, following blue and white arrows.

24 Follow blue arrows through residential roads of Mid Lavant. At 'square' turn **L** then **L** again to continue in same direction. Pass between concrete bollards then as road swings right bear **L** on Churchmead Close 'Chichester'. Shortly bear **L** again on Warbleheath Close following 'Centurion Way' signs.

25 Follow Centurion Way for 3¼ miles passing metal sculptures of Roman soldiers. At T-j with road at end of cyclepath turn **L** to rejoin outward route 'City centre ¾'.

26 At small roundabout **SA** on Westgate 'South Coast Cycle Route'. At large roundabout take third exit on West Street to return to Chichester Cathedral.

1 With your back to Chichester Cathedral turn **L** along West Street. At large roundabout take second exit '7.5 ton weight limit' on road paved with red bricks.

2 At mini-roundabout continue in same direction on Westgate Street 'South Coast Cycle Route' (denoted from now on as 'SCCR'). Follow to end of road towards metal fencing and go over level crossing. At T-j bear **R**.

3 After ¼ mile, shortly after passing Appledram Lane on left, next **R** on Clay Lane 'SCCR'.

4 Go over second level crossing, pass under A27. At X-roads with Salthill Road **SA** on continuation of Clay Lane.

5 After almost 2 miles, ignore left turn (Ratham Lane). Shortly after sharp right-hand bend next **L** on Southbrook Road.

6 At T-j turn **L** 'Hambrook, SCCR'.

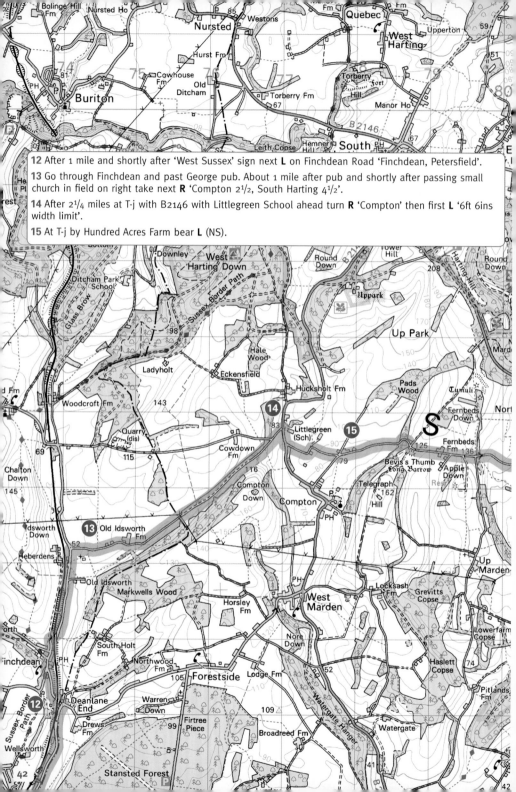

12 After 1 mile and shortly after 'West Sussex' sign next **L** on Finchdean Road 'Finchdean, Petersfield'.

13 Go through Finchdean and past George pub. About 1 mile after pub and shortly after passing small church in field on right take next **R** 'Compton 2½, South Harting 4½'.

14 After 2¼ miles at T-j with B2146 with Littlegreen School ahead turn **R** 'Compton' then first **L** '6ft 6ins width limit'.

15 At T-j by Hundred Acres Farm bear **L** (NS).

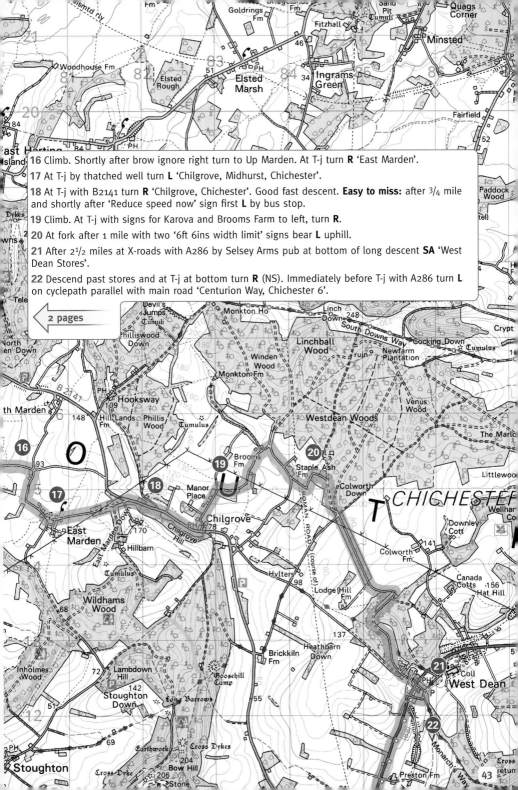

16 Climb. Shortly after brow ignore right turn to Up Marden. At T-j turn **R** 'East Marden'.

17 At T-j by thatched well turn **L** 'Chilgrove, Midhurst, Chichester'.

18 At T-j with B2141 turn **R** 'Chilgrove, Chichester'. Good fast descent. **Easy to miss:** after 3/4 mile and shortly after 'Reduce speed now' sign first **L** by bus stop.

19 Climb. At T-j with signs for Karova and Brooms Farm to left, turn **R**.

20 At fork after 1 mile with two '6ft 6ins width limit' signs bear **L** uphill.

21 After 2½ miles at X-roads with A286 by Selsey Arms pub at bottom of long descent **SA** 'West Dean Stores'.

22 Descend past stores and at T-j at bottom turn **R** (NS). Immediately before T-j with A286 turn **L** on cyclepath parallel with main road 'Centurion Way, Chichester 6'.

2 pages

Rolling woodland between Cranleigh & Chiddingfold

The Downs Link is a traffic-free trail on the course of a dismantled railway that runs through Cranleigh and offers a convenient alternative to busy roads if you are heading north. Be warned that although it is a broad stone-based track it can be muddy in winter or after prolonged rain. A private road with bridleway status forms a fine link from the railway path to the quiet lanes that meander through to Thorncombe Street. Just south of here lies Winkworth Arboretum with 100 acres of hillside covered in azaleas

and bluebells, best seen in spring and autumn. There is also a tearoom here. For further details go to www. nationaltrust.org.uk/main/ w-winkwortharboretum. The longest and steepest climb of the day leads west from Hascombe to Hydestile. Wooded lanes connect the villages and pubs of Hambledon, Chiddingfold and Dunsfold. An unavoidable but thankfully short section of the busy A281 north of Alfold Crossways takes you back towards Cranleigh where you can choose between tarmac or traffic-free trail to return

you to the start. If you have hybrid or mountain bikes you can follow the whole length of the traffic-free Downs Link for 30 miles from the A248 at Peasmarsh (south of Guildford) all the way to Old Shoreham near the South Coast. The ride is predominantly on the course of an old railway but there are linking sections on quiet roads and tracks. For more details go to www.westsussex.gov.uk and follow links through 'Leisure & Tourism' then 'Walking, Cycling and Horseriding' to get to 'Downs Link'.

Overview
On-road ● 27 miles / 43 kilometres ● Easy / Moderate

Start & Parking
Village Way Pay & Display car park by Cranleigh Leisure Centre (off the High Street, opposite the main post office)

Busy roads
● 250yds on A281 northwest of Cranleigh **4**

● 1/2 mile on A281 north of Alfold Crossways with a difficult right turn **15**

Off-road sections
The Downs Link is used at the start and finish. Although stone-based there may be occasional muddy sections after prolonged rain and through the winter

Terrain
Several 100-200ft (30-60m) climbs and one longer, steeper one

Other rides nearby

Ride 7

Ride 8
Page 50

Ride 9
Page 56

Nearest railway
Witley, just west of Hambledon

Refreshments
Cranleigh
Lots of choice

**Hascombe
(just off the route)**
White Horse PH
T: 01483 208258

Hambledon
Merry Harriers PH
T: 01428 682883

Chiddingfold
Crown PH
T: 01428 682255
Swan Inn
T: 01428 682073

Dunsfold
Sun Inn
T: 01483 200242

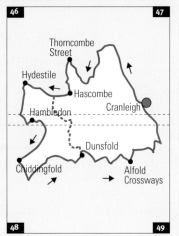

Map pages

46

47

Thorncombe
Street

Hydestile

Hascombe

Hambledon

Cranleigh

Dunsfold

Chiddingfold

Alfold
Crossways

48

49

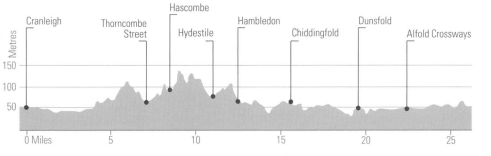

Metres

Cranleigh

Thorncombe
Street

Hascombe

Hydestile

Hambledon

Chiddingfold

Dunsfold

Alfold Crossways

150

100

50

0 Miles   5   10   15   20   25

4 Soon join tarmac then at T-j with busy A281 turn **R** (use pavement) then first **L** immediately before 'Birtley Green' sign on tarmac bridleway 'Private Road'.

5 Follow lane past houses. At T-j by 'Gate Street Barn' sign turn **L**.

6 At next T-j after ½ mile turn **R** uphill 'Thorncombe 2, Godalming 5'.

7 After 1¾ miles, shortly after passing lovely honey-coloured, half-timbered Thorncombe House turn first **L** 'Arboretum, Hascombe'.

8 At T-j with The Street (B2130) at top of Lodkin Hill turn **L**. Descend then climb. Soon after start of houses first **R** on Mare Lane '6ft 6ins width limit'.

9 Steep climb on narrow (muddy) lane. At T-j by triangle of grass turn **R** (NS) to continue gently uphill.

10 Ignore right turn to Godalming. At X-roads (Give Way) by brick bus shelter turn **L** 'Hambledon, Chiddingfold'.

11 After 1¼ miles ignore first left to Hambledon Church. Climb to top of hill then shortly after start of descent next **L** on Woodlands Road 'Pockford, Dunsfold'. At T-j with Vann Lane at end of Woodlands Road turn **L** 'Surrey Cycleway'.

2 pages

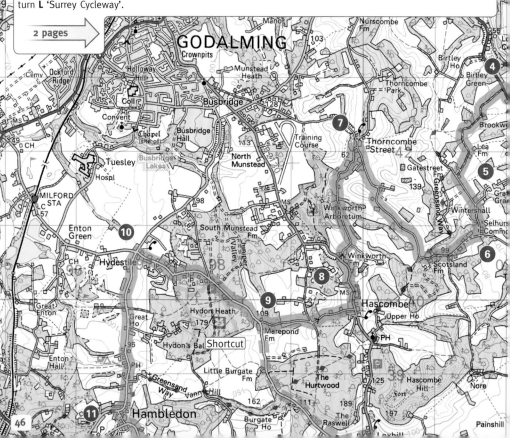

1 Exit Village Way car park and turn **L** past Leisure Centre along cul-de-sac with double yellow lines and on narrow tarmac track.

2 Cross narrow bridge, turn **R** then **R** again on wider bridge following broad gravel track between wooden posts. At T-j with road (Marks & Spencer to right) turn **L** on track then cross next road on continuation of Downs Link railway path.

3 Tarmac turns to track. After 1¼ miles cross bridge over small river. **Easy to miss:** after further 1½ miles, at third round red-brick bridge (with wooden bench to right) turn **L** away from railway path up steps to wide gravel track. Turn **R** towards barns along line of telegraph poles.

Ride 8 also starts at Cranleigh. Page 50

47

11 After 1¼ miles ignore first left to Hambledon Church. Climb to top of hill then shortly after start of descent next **L** on Woodlands Road 'Pockford, Dunsfold'. At T-j with Vann Lane at end of Woodlands Road turn **L** 'Surrey Cycleway'.

12 After 3½ miles at T-j in Chiddingfold at end of Pockford Road turn **L** on Pickhurst Road (or turn **R** for refreshments in Chiddingfold).

13 After 1 mile first **L** on High Street Green 'Dunsfold, Cranleigh'.

14 After 3 miles, at X-roads (your priority) by memorial cross in Dunsfold, shortly after '40mph' signs and opposite Sun pub (off to left), turn **R** on Alfold Road 'Alfold, Horsham'.

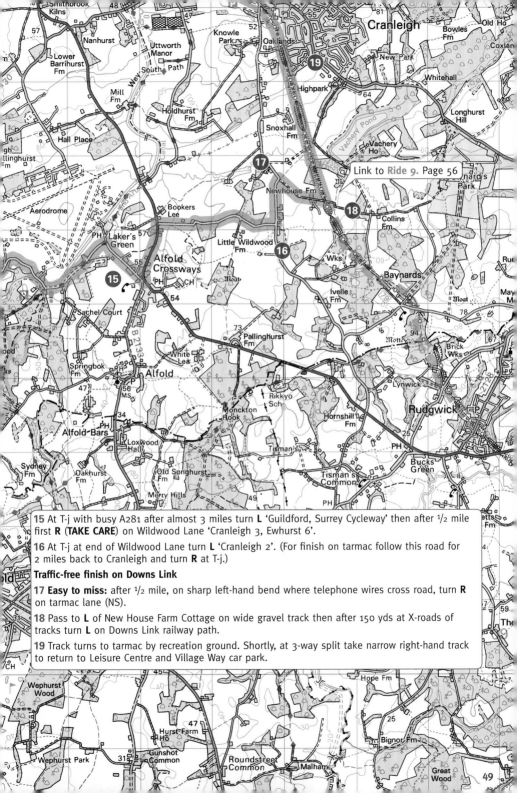

Link to **Ride 9.** Page 56

15 At T-j with busy A281 after almost 3 miles turn **L** 'Guildford, Surrey Cycleway' then after 1/2 mile first **R** (**TAKE CARE**) on Wildwood Lane 'Cranleigh 3, Ewhurst 6'.

16 At T-j at end of Wildwood Lane turn **L** 'Cranleigh 2'. (For finish on tarmac follow this road for 2 miles back to Cranleigh and turn **R** at T-j.)

Traffic-free finish on Downs Link

17 Easy to miss: after 1/2 mile, on sharp left-hand bend where telephone wires cross road, turn **R** on tarmac lane (NS).

18 Pass to **L** of New House Farm Cottage on wide gravel track then after 150 yds at X-roads of tracks turn **L** on Downs Link railway path.

19 Track turns to tarmac by recreation ground. Shortly, at 3-way split take narrow right-hand track to return to Leisure Centre and Village Way car park.

East from Cranleigh into the Surrey Hills

The highlight of this ride is undoubtedly the beautiful woodland cloaking the hills that lie to the south of the A25 between Dorking and Guildford, seen at their best in late spring with carpets of bluebells and almost translucent green leaves, or in late autumn with the leaves changing in a riot of colour, a last surge of life before the oncoming darker months. All this comes in the second half of the ride. At the start you have a choice of the traffic-free Downs Link, an old railway path converted to recreational use, or the parallel road. Although the traffic-free path would seem the obvious choice, be warned that you will face big puddles and some mud in the winter and after prolonged rain at any time of year, so it is not suitable for lightweight road bikes. After a few miles of gently undulating lanes you are faced with the first big climb up towards Leith Hill (at 965ft (294m) this is the highest point in South East England). If it is a clear day you may wish to push your bikes up the bridleway that leads to the 18th century tower with its magnificent panoramic views. The tower was built by local landowner Richard Hull – he was buried upside down beneath the tower, believing that the world would spin round so that on Judgement Day he would be facing his Maker. Descend to Peaslake where the takeaway teas and cakes from the Peaslake Stores can revive tired legs. A second long climbs leads up through the delights of Winterfold Wood before the long descent back to Cranleigh.

Overview

On-road ● 23 miles / 37 kilometres ● Moderate / Strenuous

Start & Parking
Village Way Pay & Display car park in Cranleigh by the Leisure Centre (off the High Street, opposite the main post office). Cranleigh lies southeast of Guildford

Busy roads
1/2 mile on the B2128 through Cranleigh (30mph speed limit) **20**

Off-road sections
Option of using the Downs Link railway path for almost 3 miles at the start (muddy in winter and after rain) **1B**

Terrain
Gently undulating in southern half of ride, hilly through woodland in the northern half with two major climbs

Nearest railway
Gomshall

Refreshments
Cranleigh
Lots of choice

Walliswood
Scarlett Arms PH
T: 01306 627243

Forest Green
Parrot Inn
T: 01306 621339

Abinger Common
Abinger Hatch PH
T: 01306 730737

Sutton Abinger
Volunteer PH
T: 01306 730798

Peaslake
Hurtwood Inn
T: 01306 730851
Peaslake Stores also serves hot drinks and snacks

Other rides nearby

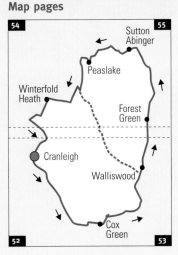

Map pages

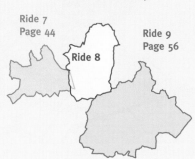

Ride 7
Page 44

Ride 9
Page 56

Ride 8

Sutton Abinger

Peaslake

Winterfold Heath

Forest Green

Cranleigh

Walliswood

Cox Green

54   55

52   53

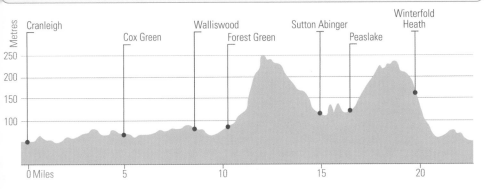

Winterfold Heath

Cranleigh

Cox Green

Walliswood

Forest Green

Sutton Abinger

Peaslake

Metres

250
200
150
100

0 Miles   5   10   15   20

51

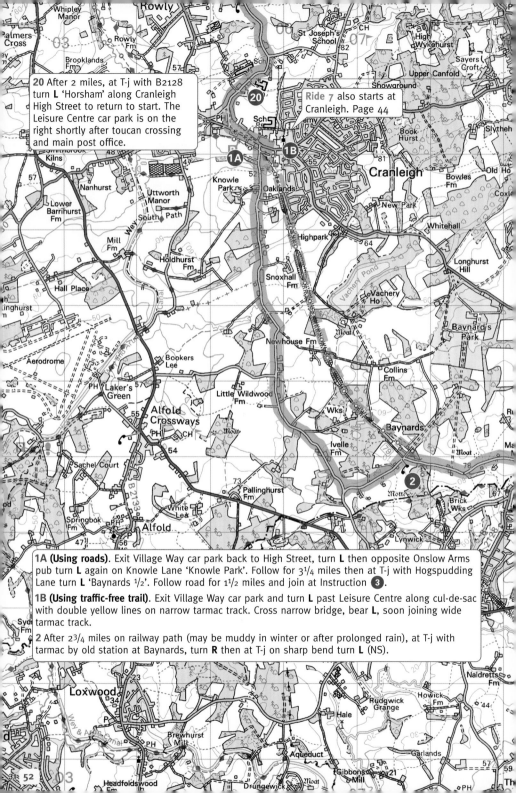

20 After 2 miles, at T-j with B2128 turn **L** 'Horsham' along Cranleigh High Street to return to start. The Leisure Centre car park is on the right shortly after toucan crossing and main post office.

Ride **7** also starts at Cranleigh. Page 44

1A (Using roads). Exit Village Way car park back to High Street, turn **L** then opposite Onslow Arms pub turn **L** again on Knowle Lane 'Knowle Park'. Follow for 3¼ miles then at T-j with Hogspudding Lane turn **L** 'Baynards ½'. Follow road for 1½ miles and join at Instruction **3**.

1B (Using traffic-free trail). Exit Village Way car park and turn **L** past Leisure Centre along cul-de-sac with double yellow lines on narrow tarmac track. Cross narrow bridge, bear **L**, soon joining wide tarmac track.

2 After 2¾ miles on railway path (may be muddy in winter or after prolonged rain), at T-j with tarmac by old station at Baynards, turn **R** then at T-j on sharp bend turn **L** (NS).

52

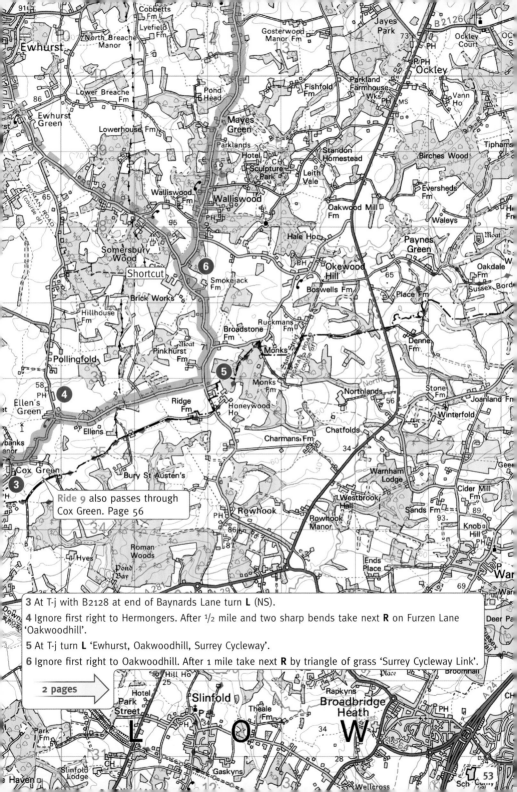

Shortcut

Ride 9 also passes through Cox Green. Page 56

3 At T-j with B2128 at end of Baynards Lane turn **L** (NS).

4 Ignore first right to Hermongers. After ½ mile and two sharp bends take next **R** on Furzen Lane 'Oakwoodhill'.

5 At T-j turn **L** 'Ewhurst, Oakwoodhill, Surrey Cycleway'.

6 Ignore first right to Oakwoodhill. After 1 mile take next **R** by triangle of grass 'Surrey Cycleway Link'.

2 pages →

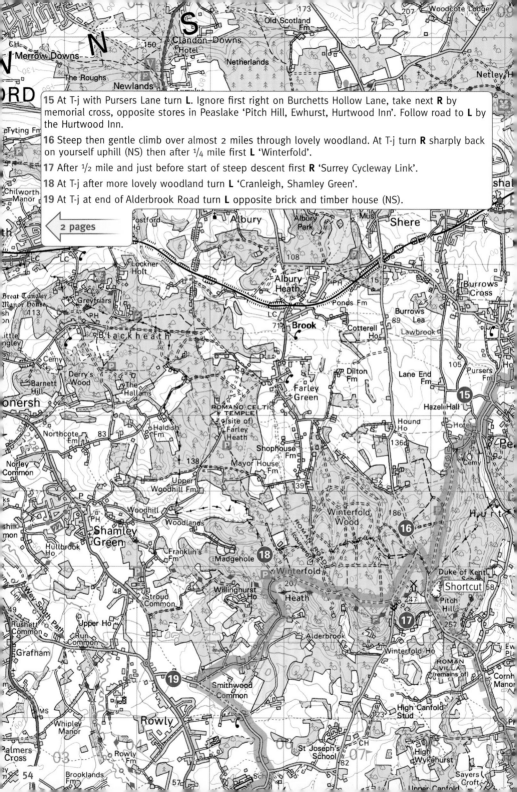

15 At T-j with Pursers Lane turn **L**. Ignore first right on Burchetts Hollow Lane, take next **R** by memorial cross, opposite stores in Peaslake 'Pitch Hill, Ewhurst, Hurtwood Inn'. Follow road to **L** by the Hurtwood Inn.

16 Steep then gentle climb over almost 2 miles through lovely woodland. At T-j turn **R** sharply back on yourself uphill (NS) then after ¼ mile first **L** 'Winterfold'.

17 After ½ mile and just before start of steep descent first **R** 'Surrey Cycleway Link'.

18 At T-j after more lovely woodland turn **L** 'Cranleigh, Shamley Green'.

19 At T-j at end of Alderbrook Road turn **L** opposite brick and timber house (NS).

← 2 pages

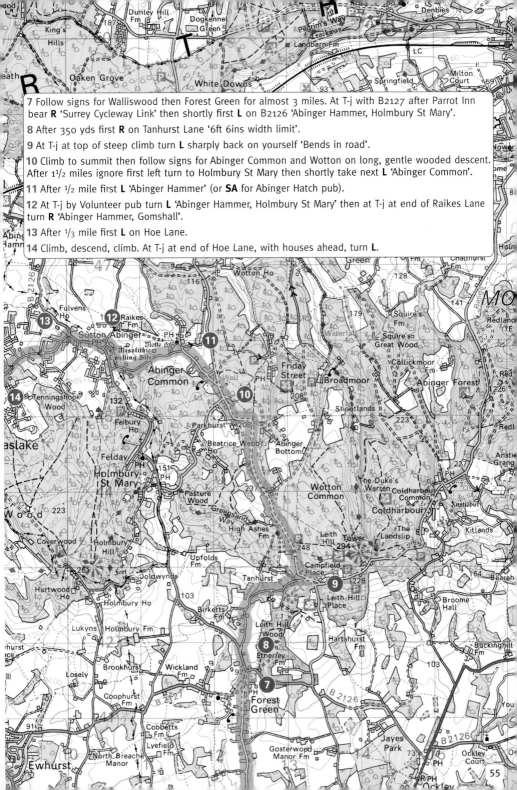

7 Follow signs for Walliswood then Forest Green for almost 3 miles. At T-j with B2127 after Parrot Inn bear **R** 'Surrey Cycleway Link' then shortly first **L** on B2126 'Abinger Hammer, Holmbury St Mary'.

8 After 350 yds first **R** on Tanhurst Lane '6ft 6ins width limit'.

9 At T-j at top of steep climb turn **L** sharply back on yourself 'Bends in road'.

10 Climb to summit then follow signs for Abinger Common and Wotton on long, gentle wooded descent. After 1½ miles ignore first left turn to Holmbury St Mary then shortly take next **L** 'Abinger Common'.

11 After ½ mile first **L** 'Abinger Hammer' (or **SA** for Abinger Hatch pub).

12 At T-j by Volunteer pub turn **L** 'Abinger Hammer, Holmbury St Mary' then at T-j at end of Raikes Lane turn **R** 'Abinger Hammer, Gomshall'.

13 After ⅓ mile first **L** on Hoe Lane.

14 Climb, descend, climb. At T-j at end of Hoe Lane, with houses ahead, turn **L**.

A ring around Horsham from Southwater

This ride seems to defy its location: running between the large conurbations of Horsham and Crawley, less than 10 miles from Gatwick, and crossing seven A roads, this is nevertheless a gem of a route, linking long sections of delightfully quiet lanes. The ride is an exploration of both the Low Weald in the west, bounded by the Arun Valley, and the higher land around St Leonard's Forest in the east. The streams flowing north from St Leonard's Forest are known as brooks and eventually form the River Mole. Those flowing south are called gills and form the River Arun. The forest ridge is therefore the watershed between the Thames and the South Coast. The ride crosses Stane Street, the Roman road that linked Chichester to London; its course is used by the A29 to the north of Billingshurst and is shown as a dead straight red line on the map. Elsewhere its course has been lost, lying under the Wealden clays. These heavy clays meant that the Low Weald was developed later than the easier, more fertile soils to the south and east, although the brickworks in the area testify to the use made of the material. Through the 16th and 17th centuries the Wealden economy boomed with the development of local ironworks, using local iron ore and charcoal from local woodland. The railway from Guildford to Horsham ran for 100 years from 1865 to 1965 and is now a traffic-free trail known as the Downs Link, suitable for mountain bikes. For more details see Ride 7.

Overview
On-road ● 36 miles / 58 kilometres ● Moderate

Start
Southwater Sports Club, at the junction of Church Lane and Worthing Road. Southwater lies south of Horsham

Parking
At Sports Club or at Southwater Country Park (along Station Road / Cripplegate Lane)

Busy roads
● 2 miles on B2128 through Rudgwick **19**

● 200yds on A281 south of Rudgwick **20**

● 1/2 mile on the A29 (pavement) to the west of Southwater **24**

Off-road sections
None

Terrain
Highest in the east in St Leonards Forest, lowest in the west in the Arun Valley, undulating in between. Several climbs of 100-200ft (30-60m) and one longer one

Nearest railway
Faygate

Refreshments
Southwater
Hen & Chicken PH
T: 01403 730349

Colgate
Dragon PH
T: 01293 851206

Faygate
Holmbush Inn
T: 01293 851539

Between Faygate and Capel
Royal Oak PH
T: 01293 871393

Okewood Hill (Oakwoodhill)
Punchbowl Inn
T: 01306 627249

Rudgwick
Kings Head PH
T: 01403 822200

The Haven
Blue Ship PH
T: 01403 822709

Map pages

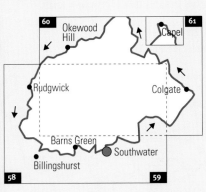

Other rides nearby

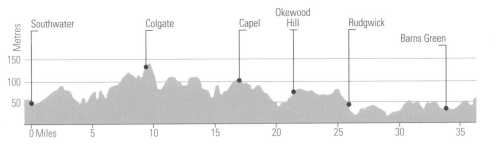

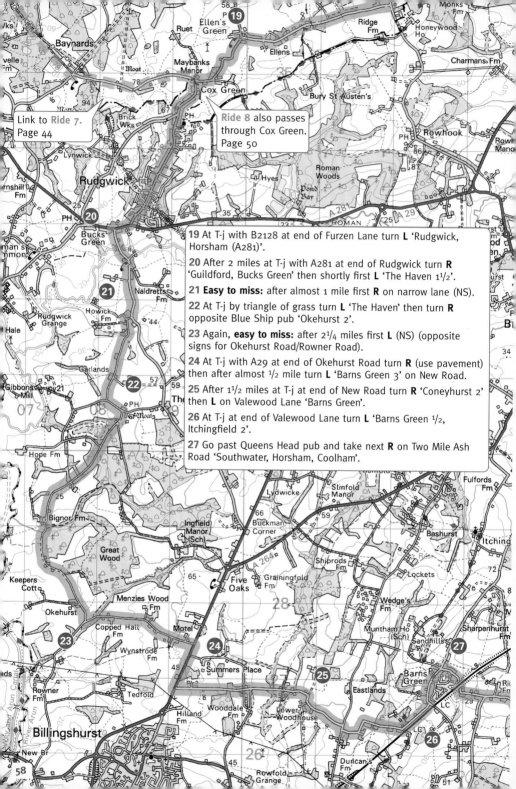

19 Monks Fm

Ride Fm
Honeywood Ho

Baynards
Ellen's Green
Ruet
Ellens
Charmans. Fm
velle
Moat
Maybanks Manor
Cox Green
Bury St Austen's
Rowhook
Rowh Mano

Link to **Ride 7.** Page 44

Ride 8 also passes through Cox Green. Page 50

Lynwick
PH
Roman Woods
Pond Bay
Hyes

rnshill Fm
Rudgwick
PH **20**
Bucks Green
ROMAN A281 A 29

man st nmon
21
Naldretts Fm
Howick Fm

Rudgwick Grange
Hale
Garlands
Gibbons Mill 21
22
Hope Fm
Moat

19 At T-j with B2128 at end of Furzen Lane turn **L** 'Rudgwick, Horsham (A281)'.

20 After 2 miles at T-j with A281 at end of Rudgwick turn **R** 'Guildford, Bucks Green' then shortly first **L** 'The Haven 1½'.

21 Easy to miss: after almost 1 mile first **R** on narrow lane (NS).

22 At T-j by triangle of grass turn **L** 'The Haven' then turn **R** opposite Blue Ship pub 'Okehurst 2'.

23 Again, **easy to miss:** after 2¼ miles first **L** (NS) (opposite signs for Okehurst Road/Rowner Road).

24 At T-j with A29 at end of Okehurst Road turn **R** (use pavement) then after almost ½ mile turn **L** 'Barns Green 3' on New Road.

25 After 1½ miles at T-j at end of New Road turn **R** 'Coneyhurst 2' then **L** on Valewood Lane 'Barns Green'.

26 At T-j at end of Valewood Lane turn **L** 'Barns Green ½, Itchingfield 2'.

27 Go past Queens Head pub and take next **R** on Two Mile Ash Road 'Southwater, Horsham, Coolham'.

Fulfords Fm
Lydwicke
Slinfold Manor
Bignor Fm
Ingfield Manor (Sch)
Buckman Corner
Bashurst
Itching
Great Wood
Shiprods Fm
Lockets
Keepers Cott
Five Oaks
Grainingfold Fm
Menzies Wood
Wedge's Fm
Okehurst
Motel
Muntham Ho (Sch)
Sharpenhurst Fm
23
Copped Hall Fm
24
Wynstrode Fm
Summers Place
27
Sandhills
Tedfold
25
Barns Green
Eastlands
Rowner Fm
Wooddale Fm
Hilland Fm
Lower Woodhouse
Billingshurst
26
New Br
Rowfold Grange
Duncan's Fm

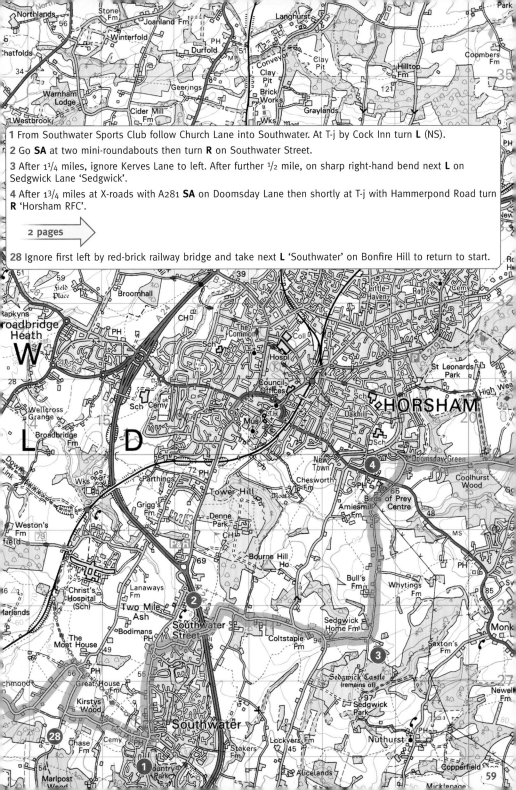

1 From Southwater Sports Club follow Church Lane into Southwater. At T-j by Cock Inn turn **L** (NS).

2 Go **SA** at two mini-roundabouts then turn **R** on Southwater Street.

3 After 1¼ miles, ignore Kerves Lane to left. After further ½ mile, on sharp right-hand bend next **L** on Sedgwick Lane 'Sedgwick'.

4 After 1¾ miles at X-roads with A281 **SA** on Doomsday Lane then shortly at T-j with Hammerpond Road turn **R** 'Horsham RFC'.

2 pages ➡

28 Ignore first left by red-brick railway bridge and take next **L** 'Southwater' on Bonfire Hill to return to start.

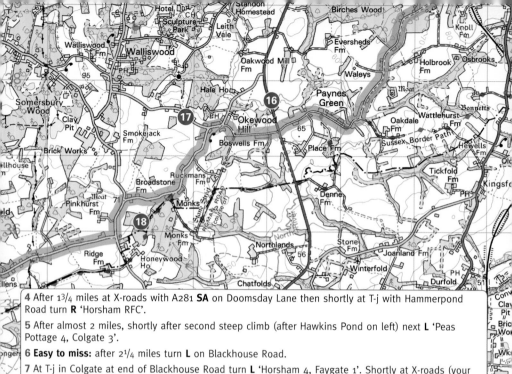

4 After 1¾ miles at X-roads with A281 **SA** on Doomsday Lane then shortly at T-j with Hammerpond Road turn **R** 'Horsham RFC'.

5 After almost 2 miles, shortly after second steep climb (after Hawkins Pond on left) next **L** 'Peas Pottage 4, Colgate 3'.

6 Easy to miss: after 2¼ miles turn **L** on Blackhouse Road.

7 At T-j in Colgate at end of Blackhouse Road turn **L** 'Horsham 4, Faygate 1'. Shortly at X-roads (your priority) turn **R** on Tower Road 'Faygate' (opposite Dragon pub).

8 At roundabout with A264 go **SA** 'Faygate, Lambs Green, Rusper' (**TAKE CARE** you may prefer to dismount and cross each lane separately).

9 Go past Holmbush Inn, cross railway bridge, climb and take first **L** on Wimlands Lane 'Wimlands 1'.

10 At T-j at end of Wimlands Lane turn **R** 'Rusper'.

11 At T-j at end of Wimland Road turn **L** then after ½ mile first **R** on Green Lane.

12 At T-j with Langhurst Wood turn **R** 'Capel 2'.

13 Go past Royal Oak pub. At T-j turn **L** 'Capel 1'.

14 After 2 miles, immediately before roundabout with A24 turn **R** on pavement, joining the Horsham Road towards Capel. Shortly first **L** on Coles Lane then at X-roads with A24 **SA** on continuation of Coles Lane (B2126) 'Ockley'.

15 Go under railway bridge then first **L** on Weare Street 'Surrey Cycleway'.

16 Follow this lovely lane for 3 miles. At X-roads with A29 at end of Weare Street **SA** on Ruckman's Lane 'Okewood, Walliswood'.

17 At T-j by telephone box and letterbox turn **L** uphill 'Surrey Cycleway'. Go past Punchbowl Inn and follow road to left.

18 At T-j turn **L** 'Horsham, Rudgwick' then after almost ½ mile first **R** 'Ellens Green, Rudgwick'.

2 pages

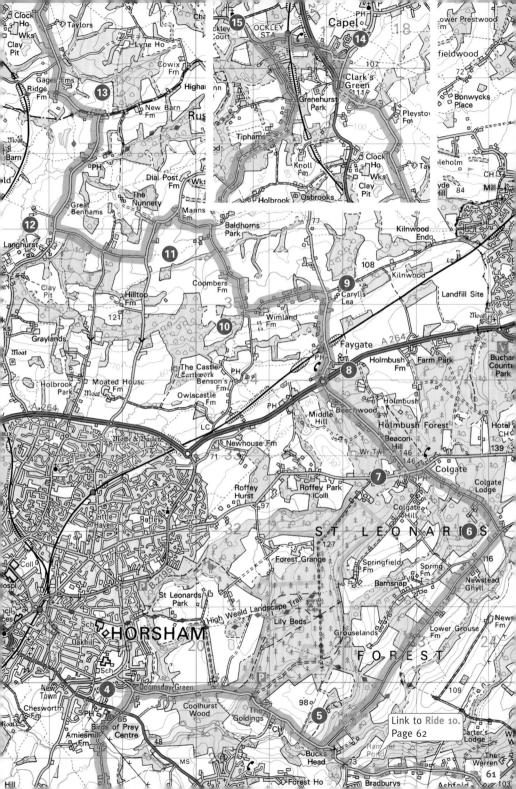

Link to **Ride 10**.
Page 62

Balcombe to the foot of the South Downs

Starting from Balcombe, a small village north of Haywards Heath, the ride plunges immediately into the heart of the attractive Sussex countryside, with steep climbs and fast descents either side of Ardingly Reservoir. The 198-acre reservoir is popular with watersports enthusiasts, anglers and birdwatchers. It feeds the River Ouse, one of the few rivers to cut through the great chalk ridge of the South Downs, passing through Lewes and emerging at the English Channel at Newhaven. Skirt around the eastern edge of Haywards Heath and soon after crossing the busy A272 the South Downs appear on the horizon. The ride heads almost due south with views towards the steep chalk escarpment, rising to 815ft (248m) on Ditchling Beacon. At one point you cross the route taken by the thousands of cyclists who take part in the London to Brighton ride each year. This ride takes a lower course along the foot of the escarpment to Clayton. As you cross the A273 bridge over the railway look to the left for a fine view of Tunnel House, a 19th century folly (complete with tunnel-keeper's cottage) built in the shape of a Tudor fortress when the railway was excavated under the South Downs. Turn north to go past the handsome buildings of Hurstpierpoint College. After crossing the valley of the infant River Ouse you are faced with the longest climb of the day north from Staplefield, setting you up with a fine long descent back down to Balcombe.

Overview
On-road ● 35 miles / 56 kilometres ● Moderate

Start
Balcombe, south of Crawley

Busy roads
Less than ¼ mile on A272
east of Haywards Heath **7**

Off-road sections
None

Terrain
Undulating with a couple of
steep 165ft (50m) climbs at
the start by Ardingly Reservoir,
several climbs of 100-200ft
(30m-60m) and one longer one

Nearest railway
Balcombe

Other rides nearby

Refreshments

Balcombe
Half Moon Inn
T: 01444 811280

Ardingly
Oak PH, Ardingly Inn
T: 01444 892244

Wivelsfield Green
Cock Inn
T: 01444 471668

Clayton
Jack & Jill Inn
T: 01273 843595

Staplefield
Victory Inn
T: 01444 400463

Map pages

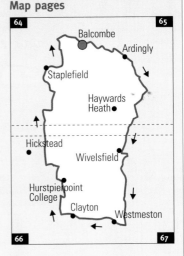

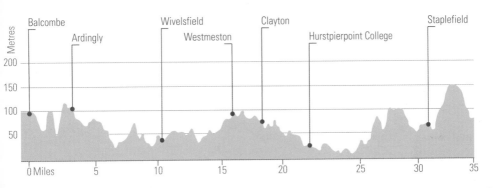

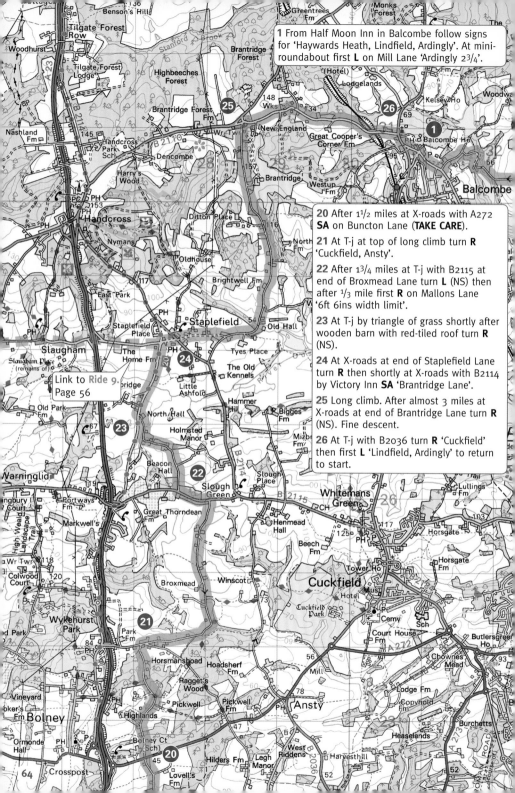

1 From Half Moon Inn in Balcombe follow signs for 'Haywards Heath, Lindfield, Ardingly'. At mini-roundabout first **L** on Mill Lane 'Ardingly 2¾'.

20 After 1½ miles at X-roads with A272 **SA** on Buncton Lane (**TAKE CARE**).

21 At T-j at top of long climb turn **R** 'Cuckfield, Ansty'.

22 After 1¾ miles at T-j with B2115 at end of Broxmead Lane turn **L** (NS) then after ⅓ mile first **R** on Mallons Lane '6ft 6ins width limit'.

23 At T-j by triangle of grass shortly after wooden barn with red-tiled roof turn **R** (NS).

24 At X-roads at end of Staplefield Lane turn **R** then shortly at X-roads with B2114 by Victory Inn **SA** 'Brantridge Lane'.

25 Long climb. After almost 3 miles at X-roads at end of Brantridge Lane turn **R** (NS). Fine descent.

26 At T-j with B2036 turn **R** 'Cuckfield' then first **L** 'Lindfield, Ardingly' to return to start.

Link to Ride 9.
Page 56

2 Descend to cross 'arm' of reservoir. Climb then descend to cross causeway across reservoir. Climb again. Go through Ardingly. At T-j turn **L** then **R** on B2028 'Lindfield, Haywards Heath'.

3 Busier section. Gentle descent. Ignore left to Highbrook. At top of gentle climb next **L** 'Horsted Keynes 2, Danehill 3½'.

4 At T-j at end of Stone Cross Lane by triangle of grass turn **R** (NS) then shortly on right-hand bend first **L** 'Freshfield 1¾, Sheffield Park 4, North Common 5'.

5 At T-j at end of Plummerden Lane turn **R** downhill by triangle of grass (NS).

Link to **Ride 11.** Page 68

6 Easy to miss: descend, cross bridge, climb past school then opposite cemetery on right turn **L** (NS). At T-j with B2111 turn **L** 'Scaynes Hill 1, Uckfield 11, Lewes 10'.

7 TAKE CARE - busy road: at T-j with A272 turn **R** then after 250 yds first **L** on Slugwash Lane '7.5 ton weight limit'.

2 pages

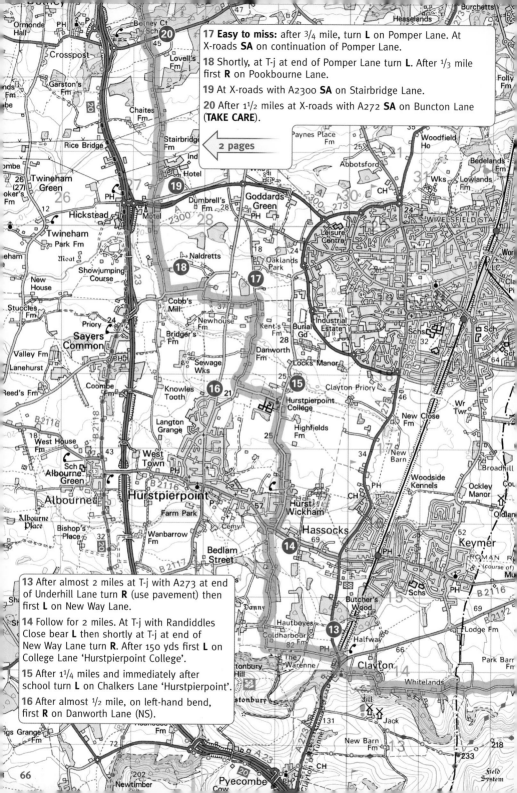

17 Easy to miss: after ¾ mile, turn **L** on Pomper Lane. At X-roads **SA** on continuation of Pomper Lane.

18 Shortly, at T-j at end of Pomper Lane turn **L**. After ⅓ mile first **R** on Pookbourne Lane.

19 At X-roads with A2300 **SA** on Stairbridge Lane.

20 After 1½ miles at X-roads with A272 **SA** on Buncton Lane (**TAKE CARE**).

2 pages

13 After almost 2 miles at T-j with A273 at end of Underhill Lane turn **R** (use pavement) then first **L** on New Way Lane.

14 Follow for 2 miles. At T-j with Randiddles Close bear **L** then shortly at T-j at end of New Way Lane turn **R**. After 150 yds first **L** on College Lane 'Hurstpierpoint College'.

15 After 1¼ miles and immediately after school turn **L** on Chalkers Lane 'Hurstpierpoint'.

16 After almost ½ mile, on left-hand bend, first **R** on Danworth Lane (NS).

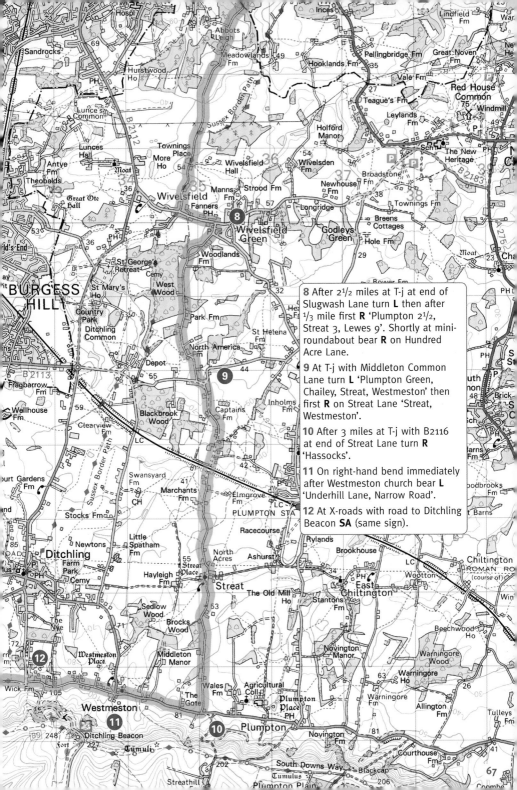

8 After 2½ miles at T-j at end of Slugwash Lane turn **L** then after ⅓ mile first **R** 'Plumpton 2½, Streat 3, Lewes 9'. Shortly at mini-roundabout bear **R** on Hundred Acre Lane.

9 At T-j with Middleton Common Lane turn **L** 'Plumpton Green, Chailey, Streat, Westmeston' then first **R** on Streat Lane 'Streat, Westmeston'.

10 After 3 miles at T-j with B2116 at end of Streat Lane turn **R** 'Hassocks'.

11 On right-hand bend immediately after Westmeston church bear **L** 'Underhill Lane, Narrow Road'.

12 At X-roads with road to Ditchling Beacon **SA** (same sign).

East Grinstead & Ashdown Forest

The Worth Way and the Forest Way are two railway paths that enable cyclists to make their way from east to west through East Grinstead avoiding the busy A22. A short section on cycle lanes and traffic-calmed streets links the two trails. Both railway paths form part of National Cycle Network Route 21 which runs from Greenwich in London down to the coast at Eastbourne. The ride heads west then south, crossing the western end of Weir Wood Reservoir and continuing

south across the wooded undulating countryside of the High Weald. It descends to its lowest point at the crossing of the River Ouse, one of the few rivers that cuts through the chalk ridge of the South Downs. The village of Fletching is almost as old as neighbouring Ashdown Forest: one village inn dates from 1150. From here you face one of the longest climbs in the whole book high up into Ashdown Forest, an area of heathland dotted with pine trees. Vast views open up looking southeast towards

the Rother Valley. Beware of sheep, which have a tendency to wander across the road with scant regard for traffic or cyclists. What goes up must come down and the descent to Forest Row comes in two parts separated by an unexpected climb up to Coleman's Hatch. Finding the alleyway that leads to the Forest Way may involve a bit of head-scratching, but from here to East Grinstead the route is clearly waymarked back to the start.

Overview

On-road ● **32 miles / 52 kilometres** ● **Moderate**

Start
East Grinstead railway station

Parking
Pay & Display car park at station

Busy roads
● ¼ mile on A22 through Nutley (30mph speed limit) **15**

● 2 miles on B2026 over the plateau of Ashdown Forest **17**

● Urban streets through East Grinstead **23** to **25**

Off-road sections
The Worth Way **1** to **2** is used at the start and the Forest Way **20** to **23** near the finish. Both are good, stone-based railway paths

Terrain
Many short climbs of 100-200ft (30-60m) and two longer ones

Nearest railway
East Grinstead

Refreshments

East Grinstead
Lots of choice

South of Horsted Keynes
Sloop PH
T: 01444 831219

Fletching
Griffin Inn
T: 01825 722890

Coleman's Hatch
Hatch Inn
T: 01342 822363

Other rides nearby

Ride 13
Page 80

Ride 11

Ride 10
Page 62

BRAMBLETYE CROSSING

Map pages

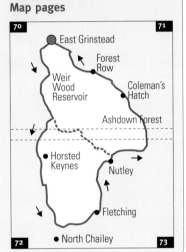

70 · East Grinstead · Forest Row · Weir Wood Reservoir · Coleman's Hatch · Ashdown Forest · Horsted Keynes · Nutley · Fletching · North Chailey · 71 · 72 · 73

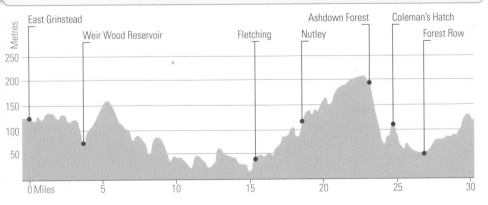

East Grinstead · Weir Wood Reservoir · Fletching · Ashdown Forest · Nutley · Coleman's Hatch · Forest Row

Metres — 250, 200, 150, 100, 50

0 Miles · 5 · 10 · 15 · 20 · 25 · 30

23 Follow for 2 miles. At next road go **SA** then at fork bear **L**. Climb. At junction with roundabout in East Grinstead turn **L** 'Town Centre Cycle Route'.

24 At mini-roundabout **SA**. At next roundabout (with London Road) turn **R** 'Worth Way, Crawley 7'. Continue **SA** at traffic lights on London Road then at next mini-roundabout by Broadway pub turn **L**.

25 At roundabout with trees in it at end of Station Approach go **SA** 'Station, Worth Way'. Follow 'NCN 21' signs in front of ticket office and up steps by red and white 'East Grinstead Railway Station' sign. Cross bridge and follow pavement to right to return to start.

1 From car park at back of East Grinstead railway station follow traffic-free path (Worth Way) directly away from station alongside car park.

2 Easy to miss: having passed under new square bridge then older round stone and brick bridge, keep an eye out for narrow gravel path to **L** sharply back on yourself gently uphill (about 1 mile from start). At T-j with road turn **R**.

3 At X-roads with B2110 at end of Imberhorne Lane **SA** on Saint Hill Road 'Saint Hill Manor'.

4 At T-j by large triangle of grass with letterbox, trees and telegraph poles turn **R** (NS).

5 Steep descent. Follow signs for West Hoathly and Horsted Keynes. Long climb. At T-j at top of Grinstead Lane turn **R** 'Sharpthorne' then shortly **L** on Chilling Street 'Courtlands Nurseries, Teas'.

2 pages ➡

18 Very fast descent then steady climb. At T-j at top of Kidds Hill by Hatch Inn turn **R** 'Forest Row 2, East Grinstead 5' then **L** downhill.

19 Shortly, at T-j with B2110 at bottom of Shepherds Gate, with church ahead, turn **L** downhill.

20 Easy to miss: descend, go round sharp left-hand bend at start of houses in Forest Row then, after ¼ mile, immediately after Stonedene Close on right and opposite Post Horn Lane on left, turn **R** on gravel track by signpost with yellow arrow on blue background. Join railway path and turn **L**.

21 Follow 'NCN 21' signs as narrow gravel track bears **R** then turns **L** on tarmac by Tablehurst Farm.

22 Cross A22 via toucan crossing then shortly go **SA** at Brambletye crossing.

Link to **Ride 13**. Page 80

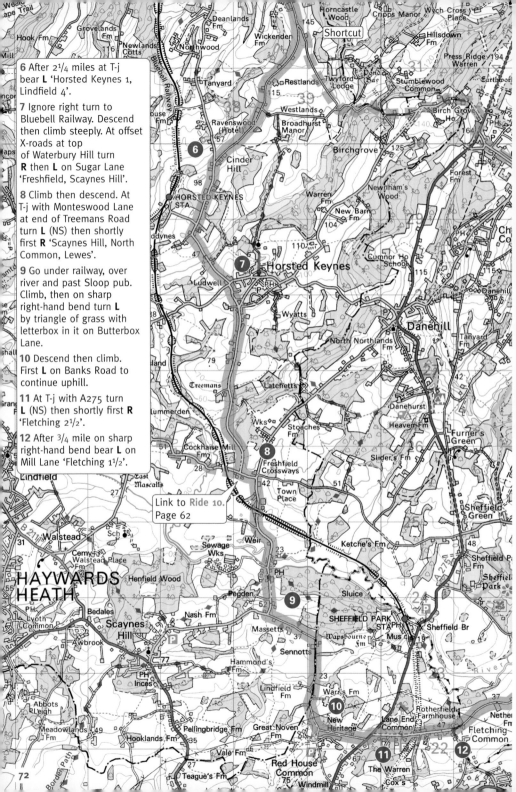

6 After 2¼ miles at T-j bear **L** 'Horsted Keynes 1, Lindfield 4'.

7 Ignore right turn to Bluebell Railway. Descend then climb steeply. At offset X-roads at top of Waterbury Hill turn **R** then **L** on Sugar Lane 'Freshfield, Scaynes Hill'.

8 Climb then descend. At T-j with Monteswood Lane at end of Treemans Road turn **L** (NS) then shortly first **R** 'Scaynes Hill, North Common, Lewes'.

9 Go under railway, over river and past Sloop pub. Climb, then on sharp right-hand bend turn **L** by triangle of grass with letterbox in it on Butterbox Lane.

10 Descend then climb. First **L** on Banks Road to continue uphill.

11 At T-j with A275 turn **L** (NS) then shortly first **R** 'Fletching 2½'.

12 After ¾ mile on sharp right-hand bend bear **L** on Mill Lane 'Fletching 1½'.

Link to **Ride 10**. Page 62

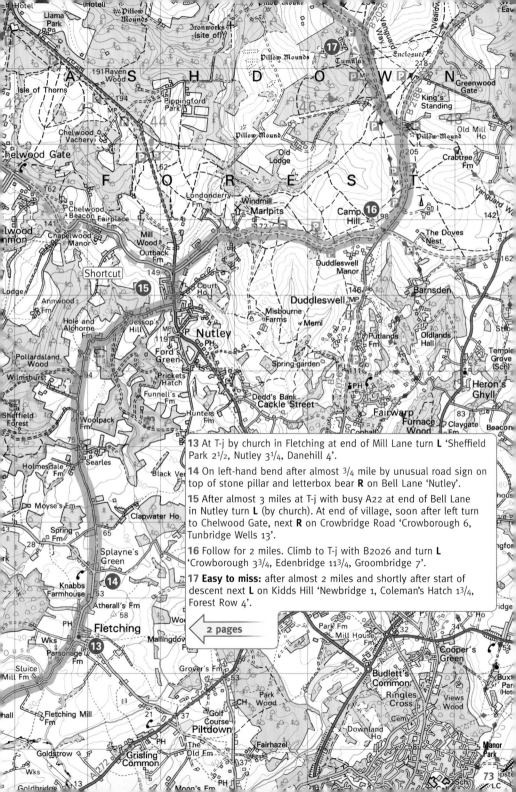

13 At T-j by church in Fletching at end of Mill Lane turn **L** 'Sheffield Park 2½, Nutley 3¼, Danehill 4'.

14 On left-hand bend after almost ¾ mile by unusual road sign on top of stone pillar and letterbox bear **R** on Bell Lane 'Nutley'.

15 After almost 3 miles at T-j with busy A22 at end of Bell Lane in Nutley turn **L** (by church). At end of village, soon after left turn to Chelwood Gate, next **R** on Crowbridge Road 'Crowborough 6, Tunbridge Wells 13'.

16 Follow for 2 miles. Climb to T-j with B2026 and turn **L** 'Crowborough 3¾, Edenbridge 11¾, Groombridge 7'.

17 Easy to miss: after almost 2 miles and shortly after start of descent next **L** on Kidds Hill 'Newbridge 1, Coleman's Hatch 1¾, Forest Row 4'.

2 pages

Edenbridge, Godstone & the North Downs

Straddling the border between Kent and Surrey, the ride starts from Edenbridge, an ancient crossing point of the River Eden, a tributary of the Medway, Kent's principal river. After a few miles of gently undulating countryside, the ride climbs up Pains Hill to the first highpoint on Limpsfield Chart. This is easy stuff compared to the next very steep climb from Titsey Church up to the highpoint of the ride by the masts on Botley Hill. At 875ft (267m) this is the highest point along the North Downs Way although it is only on the steep, wooded descent that you get the very best views of the day. The North Downs Way is a long-distance National Trail that runs for 153 miles from Farnham to Dover, largely following the chalk ridge of the North Downs through Surrey and Kent. As it passes through Canterbury it is also known as the 'Pilgrims Way'. After a long stretch without any refreshment opportunities, Godstone has several pubs

and cafés to give you a boost up over Tilburstowhill Common and down to Lingfield with its racecourse. Some of the quietest and loveliest lanes of the day run from Dormansland through Cowden and Markbeech back to Edenbridge. Lying just off the route towards the end of the ride is Hever Castle,

dating from the 13th century and famous as the childhood home of Anne Boleyn, one of Henry VIII's six wives. The American William Waldorf restored the castle in 1903, creating a spectacular Italian garden containing statuary from Roman to Renaissance times.

Overview
On-road ● 34 miles / 55 kilometres ● Moderate

Start
Centre of Edenbridge,
southwest of Sevenoaks

Parking
Large free car park at the
Leisure Centre in Edenbridge

Busy roads
A25 through Godstone (cycle
lane then 30mph speed limit)
13 to **15**

Off-road sections
None

Terrain
Undulating in the southern half
of the ride with several climbs
of 100-200ft (30-60m) and
one longer one from Lingfield.
Hilly in the north half with two
steep challenges

Nearest railway
Edenbridge

Refreshments
Edenbridge
Lots of choice

A25 near Westerham
Grasshopper Inn
T: 01959 563136

Godstone
Lots of choice

South of Godstone
Fox & Hounds PH
T: 01342 893474

Crowhurst Lane End
Brickmakers Arms PH
T: 01342 892212

Lingfield
Lots of choice

Cowden
Fountain PH
T: 01342 850258

Markbeech
Kentish Horse PH
T: 01342 850493

Hever
Greyhound PH
T: 01732 862221

Other rides nearby

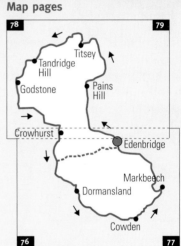

Map pages

Ride 12

Ride 13
Page 80

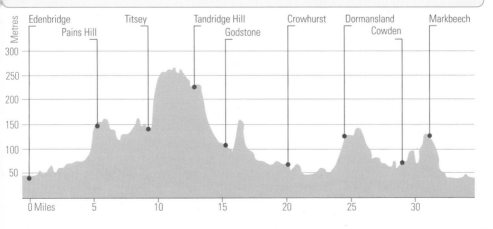

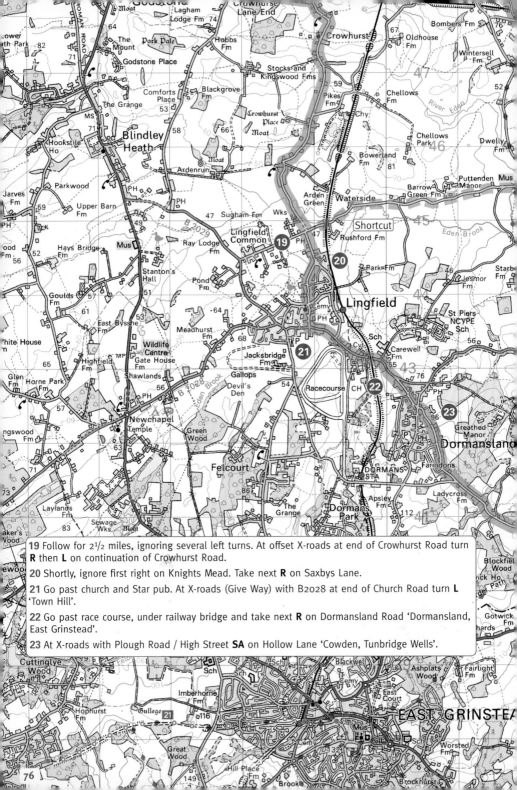

19 Follow for 2¹/₂ miles, ignoring several left turns. At offset X-roads at end of Crowhurst Road turn **R** then **L** on continuation of Crowhurst Road.

20 Shortly, ignore first right on Knights Mead. Take next **R** on Saxbys Lane.

21 Go past church and Star pub. At X-roads (Give Way) with B2028 at end of Church Road turn **L** 'Town Hill'.

22 Go past race course, under railway bridge and take next **R** on Dormansland Road 'Dormansland, East Grinstead'.

23 At X-roads with Plough Road / High Street **SA** on Hollow Lane 'Cowden, Tunbridge Wells'.

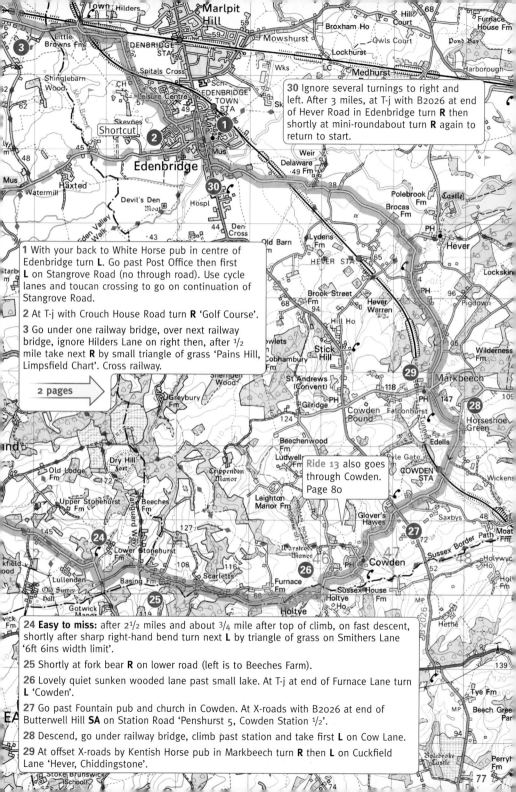

30 Ignore several turnings to right and left. After 3 miles, at T-j with B2026 at end of Hever Road in Edenbridge turn **R** then shortly at mini-roundabout turn **R** again to return to start.

1 With your back to White Horse pub in centre of Edenbridge turn **L**. Go past Post Office then first **L** on Stangrove Road (no through road). Use cycle lanes and toucan crossing to go on continuation of Stangrove Road.

2 At T-j with Crouch House Road turn **R** 'Golf Course'.

3 Go under one railway bridge, over next railway bridge, ignore Hilders Lane on right then, after ½ mile take next **R** by small triangle of grass 'Pains Hill, Limpsfield Chart'. Cross railway.

2 pages ➡

Ride **13** also goes through Cowden. Page 80

24 Easy to miss: after 2½ miles and about ¾ mile after top of climb, on fast descent, shortly after sharp right-hand bend turn next **L** by triangle of grass on Smithers Lane '6ft 6ins width limit'.

25 Shortly at fork bear **R** on lower road (left is to Beeches Farm).

26 Lovely quiet sunken wooded lane past small lake. At T-j at end of Furnace Lane turn **L** 'Cowden'.

27 Go past Fountain pub and church in Cowden. At X-roads with B2026 at end of Butterwell Hill **SA** on Station Road 'Penshurst 5, Cowden Station ½'.

28 Descend, go under railway bridge, climb past station and take first **L** on Cow Lane.

29 At offset X-roads by Kentish Horse pub in Markbeech turn **R** then **L** on Cuckfield Lane 'Hever, Chiddingstone'.

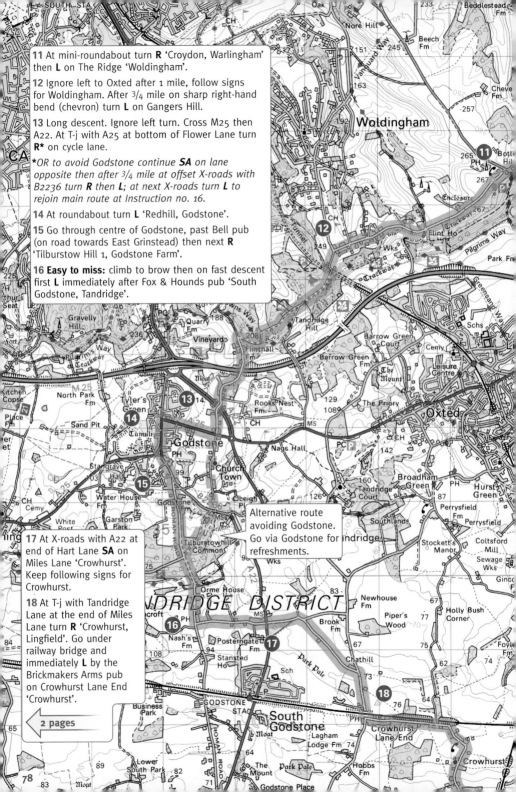

11 At mini-roundabout turn **R** 'Croydon, Warlingham' then **L** on The Ridge 'Woldingham'.

12 Ignore left to Oxted after 1 mile, follow signs for Woldingham. After 3/4 mile on sharp right-hand bend (chevron) turn **L** on Gangers Hill.

13 Long descent. Ignore left turn. Cross M25 then A22. At T-j with A25 at bottom of Flower Lane turn **R*** on cycle lane.

OR to avoid Godstone continue **SA on lane opposite then after 3/4 mile at offset X-roads with B2236 turn **R** then **L**; at next X-roads turn **L** to rejoin main route at Instruction no. 16.*

14 At roundabout turn **L** 'Redhill, Godstone'.

15 Go through centre of Godstone, past Bell pub (on road towards East Grinstead) then next **R** 'Tilburstow Hill 1, Godstone Farm'.

16 Easy to miss: climb to brow then on fast descent first **L** immediately after Fox & Hounds pub 'South Godstone, Tandridge'.

Alternative route avoiding Godstone. Go via Godstone for refreshments.

17 At X-roads with A22 at end of Hart Lane **SA** on Miles Lane 'Crowhurst'. Keep following signs for Crowhurst.

18 At T-j with Tandridge Lane at the end of Miles Lane turn **R** 'Crowhurst, Lingfield'. Go under railway bridge and immediately **L** by the Brickmakers Arms pub on Crowhurst Lane End 'Crowhurst'.

2 pages

78

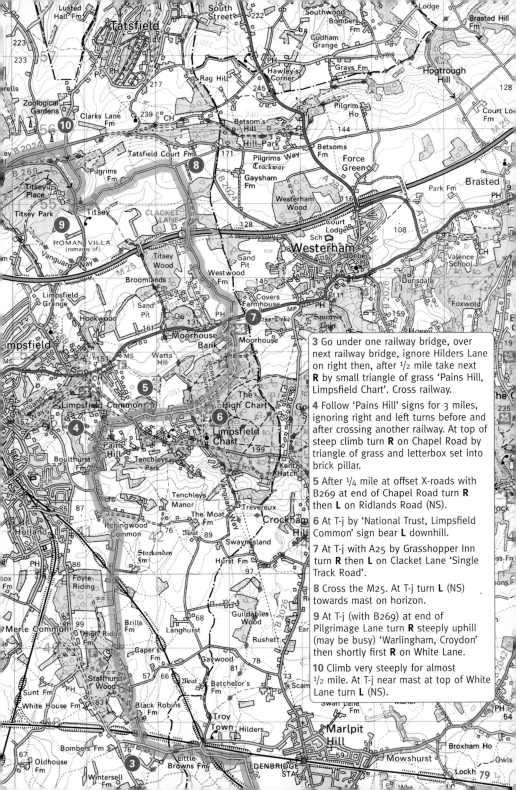

3 Go under one railway bridge, over next railway bridge, ignore Hilders Lane on right then, after ¹/₂ mile take next **R** by small triangle of grass 'Pains Hill, Limpsfield Chart'. Cross railway.

4 Follow 'Pains Hill' signs for 3 miles, ignoring right and left turns before and after crossing another railway. At top of steep climb turn **R** on Chapel Road by triangle of grass and letterbox set into brick pillar.

5 After ¹/₄ mile at offset X-roads with B269 at end of Chapel Road turn **R** then **L** on Ridlands Road (NS).

6 At T-j by 'National Trust, Limpsfield Common' sign bear **L** downhill.

7 At T-j with A25 by Grasshopper Inn turn **R** then **L** on Clacket Lane 'Single Track Road'.

8 Cross the M25. At T-j turn **L** (NS) towards mast on horizon.

9 At T-j (with B269) at end of Pilgrimage Lane turn **R** steeply uphill (may be busy) 'Warlingham, Croydon' then shortly first **R** on White Lane.

10 Climb very steeply for almost ¹/₂ mile. At T-j near mast at top of White Lane turn **L** (NS).

Groombridge & Toy's Hill

The whole of South
East England was
once covered with a
mighty dome of chalk, formed
60 million years ago by the
microscopic skeletons of
plankton when the area was
a shallow sea. Over millions

River Eden. This ride starts in
Groombridge below the high
plateau of Ashdown Forest
and weaves its way north
on a series of quiet lanes
towards the hills to the west
of Sevenoaks, passing the
glittering expanse of Bough

of the ride near to The Chart,
you drop swiftly back down to
the Low Weald with a chance
of a cultural stop at Hever
Castle, the childhood home
of Anne Boleyn. South of
the River Eden, crossed
near Hever Castle, the ride

of years the top of the dome
has been eroded, leaving
as remnants only the chalk
ridges of the North and South
Downs either side of the
exposed harder rocks of the
High Weald. In its northern
half this has been cut through
by the River Medway and one
of its principal tributaries, the

Beech Reservoir on the way.
One of the steepest climbs
in the book takes you from
the reservoir up towards
Goathurst Common, with a
particularly cruel section right
at the top. After visiting the
pretty village of Ide Hill, set
around its expansive green,
and climbing to the highpoint

climbs and descends twice,
dropping down into the
valleys formed by Kent Water
then the River Medway. Join
the traffic-free railway path
known as the Forest Way to
return to Groombridge.

Overview

On-road ● 32 miles / 52 kilometres ● Moderate / Strenuous

Start
Groombridge, west of
Tunbridge Wells

Parking
Free car park in the centre
of Groombridge

Busy roads
1/4 mile on A264 north of
Groombridge **4**

Off-road sections
The Forest Way is used for
almost 4 miles between
Hartfield and Groombridge **26**
to **27**

Terrain
Undulating with one very
steep climb up to Goathurst
Common / Ide Hill. Several
climbs of 100-200ft (30-60m)
and three longer ones

Nearest railway
Groombridge

Refreshments
Groombridge
Crown PH
T: 01892 864742

Hoath Corner
Rock PH .
T: 01892 870296

Ide Hill
Cock Inn
T: 01732 750310

Hever
King Henry VIII PH
T: 01732 862457

Markbeech
Kentish Horse PH
T: 01342 850493

Cowden
Fountain PH
T: 01342 850258

Other rides nearby

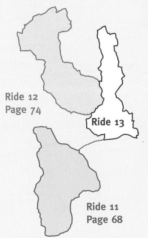

Ride 12
Page 74

Ride 13

Ride 11
Page 68

Map pages

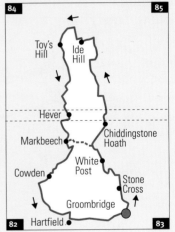

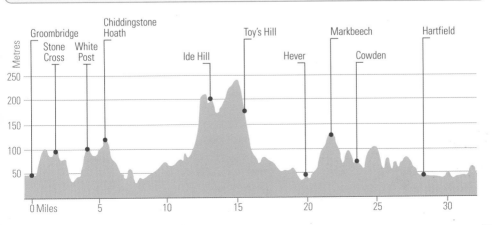

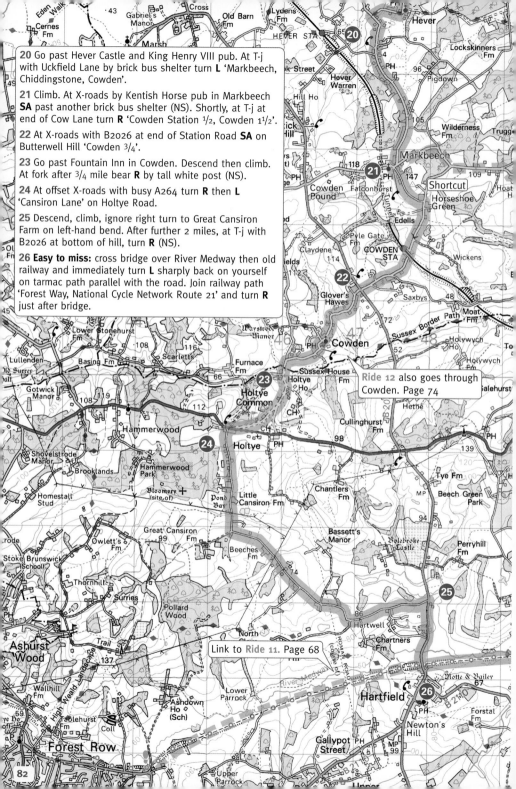

20 Go past Hever Castle and King Henry VIII pub. At T-j with Uckfield Lane by brick bus shelter turn **L** 'Markbeech, Chiddingstone, Cowden'.

21 Climb. At X-roads by Kentish Horse pub in Markbeech **SA** past another brick bus shelter (NS). Shortly, at T-j at end of Cow Lane turn **R** 'Cowden Station ½, Cowden 1½'.

22 At X-roads with B2026 at end of Station Road **SA** on Butterwell Hill 'Cowden ¾'.

23 Go past Fountain Inn in Cowden. Descend then climb. At fork after ¾ mile bear **R** by tall white post (NS).

24 At offset X-roads with busy A264 turn **R** then **L** 'Cansiron Lane' on Holtye Road.

25 Descend, climb, ignore right turn to Great Cansiron Farm on left-hand bend. After further 2 miles, at T-j with B2026 at bottom of hill, turn **R** (NS).

26 Easy to miss: cross bridge over River Medway then old railway and immediately turn **L** sharply back on yourself on tarmac path parallel with the road. Join railway path 'Forest Way, National Cycle Network Route 21' and turn **R** just after bridge.

Ride **12** also goes through Cowden. Page 74

Link to **Ride 11**. Page 68

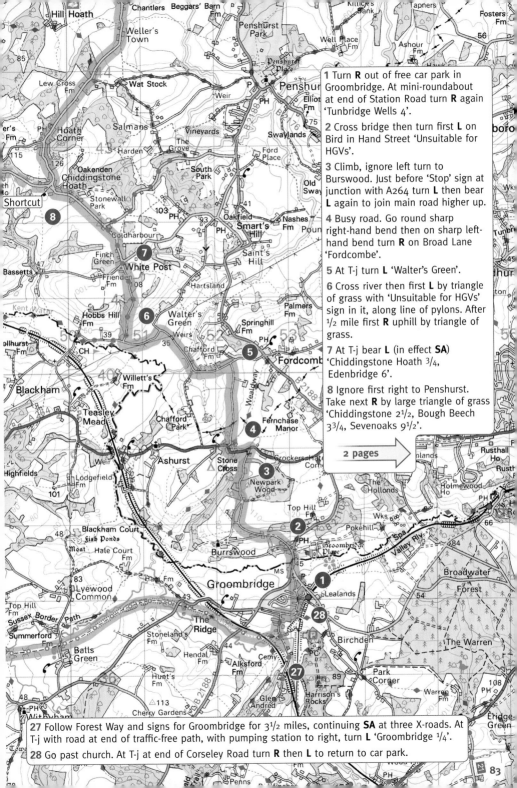

1 Turn **R** out of free car park in Groombridge. At mini-roundabout at end of Station Road turn **R** again 'Tunbridge Wells 4'.

2 Cross bridge then turn first **L** on Bird in Hand Street 'Unsuitable for HGVs'.

3 Climb, ignore left turn to Burswood. Just before 'Stop' sign at junction with A264 turn **L** then bear **L** again to join main road higher up.

4 Busy road. Go round sharp right-hand bend then on sharp left-hand bend turn **R** on Broad Lane 'Fordcombe'.

5 At T-j turn **L** 'Walter's Green'.

6 Cross river then first **L** by triangle of grass with 'Unsuitable for HGVs' sign in it, along line of pylons. After 1/2 mile first **R** uphill by triangle of grass.

7 At T-j bear **L** (in effect **SA**) 'Chiddingstone Hoath 3/4, Edenbridge 6'.

8 Ignore first right to Penshurst. Take next **R** by large triangle of grass 'Chiddingstone 21/2, Bough Beech 33/4, Sevenoaks 91/2'.

2 pages →

27 Follow Forest Way and signs for Groombridge for 31/2 miles, continuing **SA** at three X-roads. At T-j with road at end of traffic-free path, with pumping station to right, turn **L** 'Groombridge 1/4'.

28 Go past church. At T-j at end of Corseley Road turn **R** then **L** to return to car park.

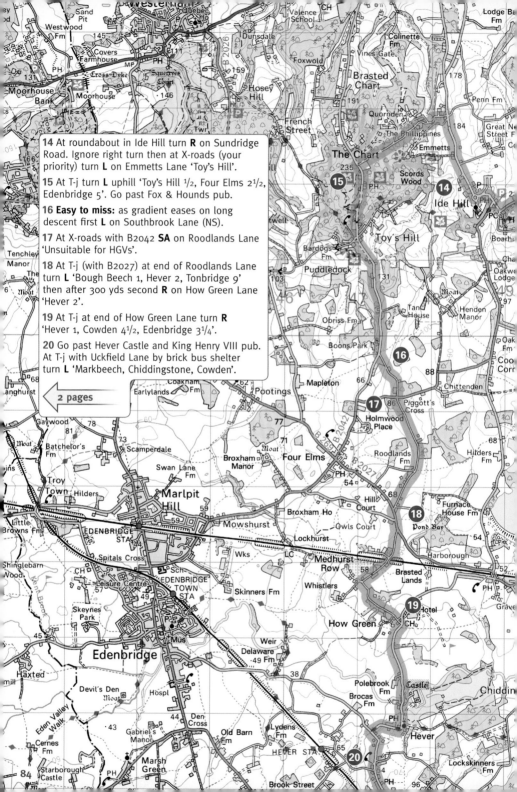

14 At roundabout in Ide Hill turn **R** on Sundridge Road. Ignore right turn then at X-roads (your priority) turn **L** on Emmetts Lane 'Toy's Hill'.

15 At T-j turn **L** uphill 'Toy's Hill ½, Four Elms 2½, Edenbridge 5'. Go past Fox & Hounds pub.

16 Easy to miss: as gradient eases on long descent first **L** on Southbrook Lane (NS).

17 At X-roads with B2042 **SA** on Roodlands Lane 'Unsuitable for HGVs'.

18 At T-j (with B2027) at end of Roodlands Lane turn **L** 'Bough Beech 1, Hever 2, Tonbridge 9' then after 300 yds second **R** on How Green Lane 'Hever 2'.

19 At T-j at end of How Green Lane turn **R** 'Hever 1, Cowden 4½, Edenbridge 3¼'.

20 Go past Hever Castle and King Henry VIII pub. At T-j with Uckfield Lane by brick bus shelter turn **L** 'Markbeech, Chiddingstone, Cowden'.

2 pages

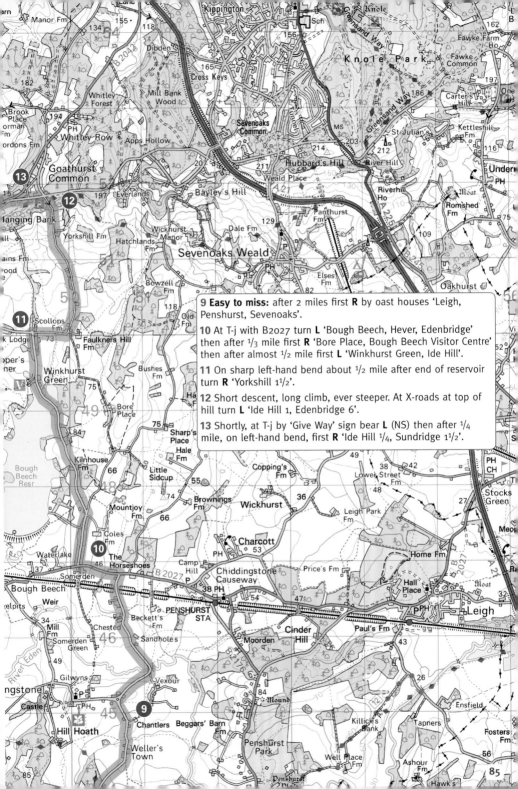

9 Easy to miss: after 2 miles first **R** by oast houses 'Leigh, Penshurst, Sevenoaks'.

10 At T-j with B2027 turn **L** 'Bough Beech, Hever, Edenbridge' then after ¹/₃ mile first **R** 'Bore Place, Bough Beech Visitor Centre' then after almost ¹/₂ mile first **L** 'Winkhurst Green, Ide Hill'.

11 On sharp left-hand bend about ¹/₂ mile after end of reservoir turn **R** 'Yorkshill 1¹/₂'.

12 Short descent, long climb, ever steeper. At X-roads at top of hill turn **L** 'Ide Hill 1, Edenbridge 6'.

13 Shortly, at T-j by 'Give Way' sign bear **L** (NS) then after ¹/₄ mile, on left-hand bend, first **R** 'Ide Hill ¹/₄, Sundridge 1¹/₂'.

From the High Weald to the Low Weald south of Uckfield

Uckfield developed as a stopping-off point on the pilgrimage route between Canterbury, Chichester and Lewes. The settlement began to develop around the bridging point of the River Uck, including the locally famous Pudding Cake Lane where travellers visited a public house for slices of pudding cake. Exposed sandstone flanks the roadside on the exit west from Uckfield, giving an indication of the underlying geology. The ride heads north crossing several tributaries of the River Ouse, which reaches the sea south of Newhaven. The first half of the route is a combination of fast descents down into the valleys followed by short steep climbs out of them. Broadleaf woodlands alternate with prosperous arable farmland. The wooded areas are reminders of the great Forest of Anderida that once extended in unbroken density from Kent to Hampshire, a distance of 120 miles. It was known to the Romans as Sylva Anderida; to the Saxons it was Andreaswald. Wolves, wild boar and deer roamed the forest. South of Hadlow the ride crosses into the area drained by Cuckmere River. Two excellent pubs in Chiddingly and Ripe may tempt you to break the ride for some refreshments before turning north back to Uckfield.

NB Do not be put off by the traffic on the first two miles out of Uckfield – this is unrepresentative of the rest of the ride, which is on much quieter roads. There simply is no other option out of Uckfield to the west and north.

Overview
On-road ● 34 miles / 55 kilometres ● Moderate

Start
Uckfield railway station, on the A22 south of East Grinstead

Parking
Several car parks in Uckfield including a large one at the Leisure Centre (north of town centre)

Busy roads
● The first two miles out of Uckfield are busy ① to ②

● ³/₄ mile on the B2192 northeast of Shortgate ㉓

● The last mile back into Uckfield is also busy ㉘

Off-road sections
None

Terrain
Hilly in the north, flatter in the south. Several climbs of 100-200ft (30-60m) and one longer one

Nearest railway
Uckfield

Refreshments
Uckfield
Lots of choice

Fairwarp
Foresters Arms PH
T: 01825 712808

High Hurstwood
Maypole Inn
T: 01825 732257

Chiddingly
Six Bells PH
T: 01825 872227

Golden Cross
Golden Cross PH
T: 01825 872216

Ripe
Lamb Inn
T: 01323 843712

Laughton
Roebuck Inn
T: 01323 811464

Other rides nearby

Ride 14

Ride 15
Page 92

Map pages

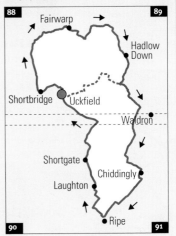

88		89
	Fairwarp →	
		Hadlow Down
Shortbridge	Uckfield	
		Waldron
	Shortgate	
		Chiddingly
	Laughton	
90		Ripe
		91

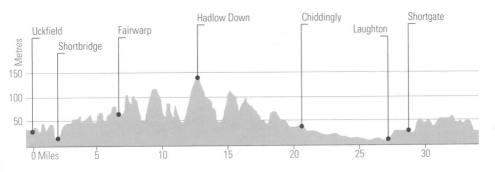

87

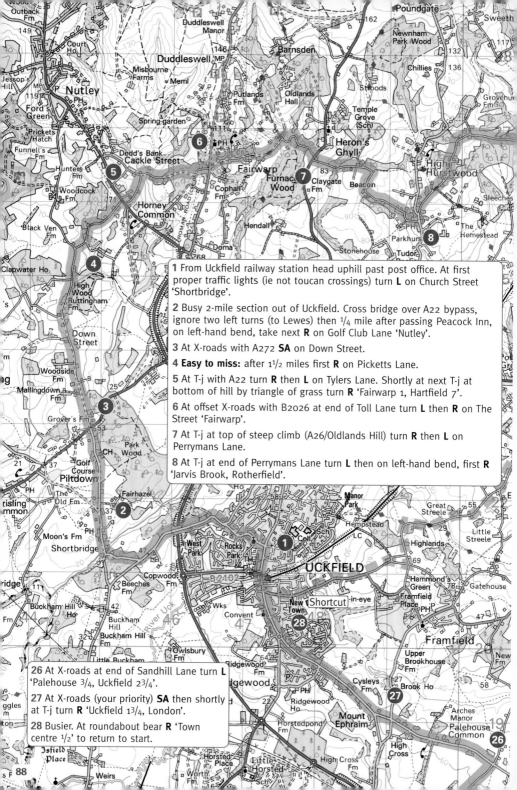

1 From Uckfield railway station head uphill past post office. At first proper traffic lights (ie not toucan crossings) turn **L** on Church Street 'Shortbridge'.

2 Busy 2-mile section out of Uckfield. Cross bridge over A22 bypass, ignore two left turns (to Lewes) then $1/4$ mile after passing Peacock Inn, on left-hand bend, take next **R** on Golf Club Lane 'Nutley'.

3 At X-roads with A272 **SA** on Down Street.

4 **Easy to miss:** after $1\frac{1}{2}$ miles first **R** on Picketts Lane.

5 At T-j with A22 turn **R** then **L** on Tylers Lane. Shortly at next T-j at bottom of hill by triangle of grass turn **R** 'Fairwarp 1, Hartfield 7'.

6 At offset X-roads with B2026 at end of Toll Lane turn **L** then **R** on The Street 'Fairwarp'.

7 At T-j at top of steep climb (A26/Oldlands Hill) turn **R** then **L** on Perrymans Lane.

8 At T-j at end of Perrymans Lane turn **L** then on left-hand bend, first **R** 'Jarvis Brook, Rotherfield'.

26 At X-roads at end of Sandhill Lane turn **L** 'Palehouse $3/4$, Uckfield $2^3/4$'.

27 At X-roads (your priority) **SA** then shortly at T-j turn **R** 'Uckfield $1^3/4$, London'.

28 Busier. At roundabout bear **R** 'Town centre $1/2$' to return to start.

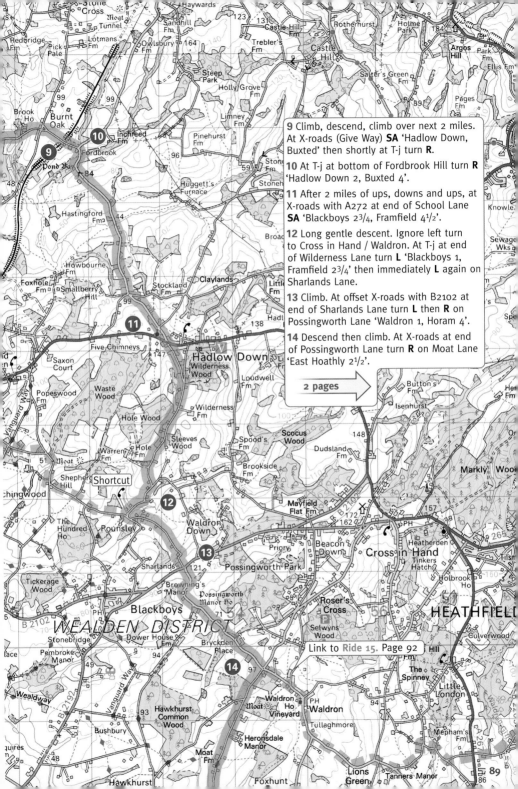

9 Climb, descend, climb over next 2 miles. At X-roads (Give Way) **SA** 'Hadlow Down, Buxted' then shortly at T-j turn **R**.

10 At T-j at bottom of Fordbrook Hill turn **R** 'Hadlow Down 2, Buxted 4'.

11 After 2 miles of ups, downs and ups, at X-roads with A272 at end of School Lane **SA** 'Blackboys 2³/₄, Framfield 4¹/₂'.

12 Long gentle descent. Ignore left turn to Cross in Hand / Waldron. At T-j at end of Wilderness Lane turn **L** 'Blackboys 1, Framfield 2³/₄' then immediately **L** again on Sharlands Lane.

13 Climb. At offset X-roads with B2102 at end of Sharlands Lane turn **L** then **R** on Possingworth Lane 'Waldron 1, Horam 4'.

14 Descend then climb. At X-roads at end of Possingworth Lane turn **R** on Moat Lane 'East Hoathly 2¹/₂'.

2 pages →

Link to **Ride 15**. Page 92

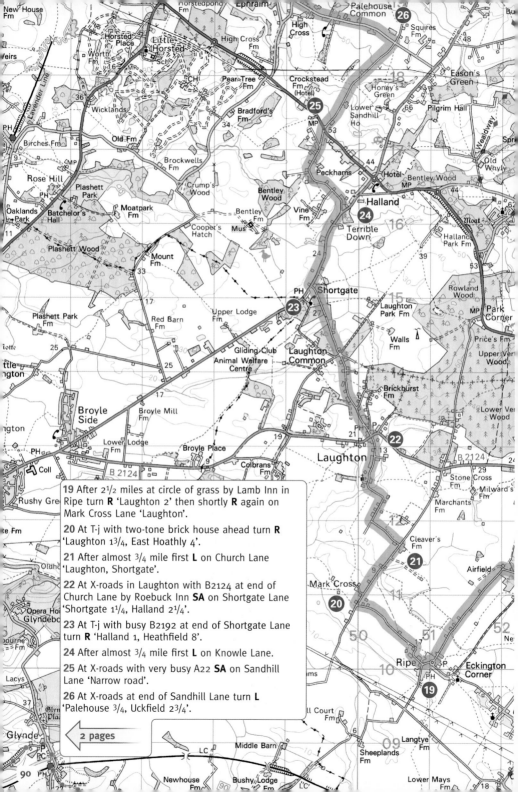

19 After 2½ miles at circle of grass by Lamb Inn in Ripe turn **R** 'Laughton 2' then shortly **R** again on Mark Cross Lane 'Laughton'.

20 At T-j with two-tone brick house ahead turn **R** 'Laughton 1¾, East Hoathly 4'.

21 After almost ¾ mile first **L** on Church Lane 'Laughton, Shortgate'.

22 At X-roads in Laughton with B2124 at end of Church Lane by Roebuck Inn **SA** on Shortgate Lane 'Shortgate 1¼, Halland 2¼'.

23 At T-j with busy B2192 at end of Shortgate Lane turn **R** 'Halland 1, Heathfield 8'.

24 After almost ¾ mile first **L** on Knowle Lane.

25 At X-roads with very busy A22 **SA** on Sandhill Lane 'Narrow road'.

26 At X-roads at end of Sandhill Lane turn **L** 'Palehouse ¾, Uckfield 2¾'.

← **2 pages**

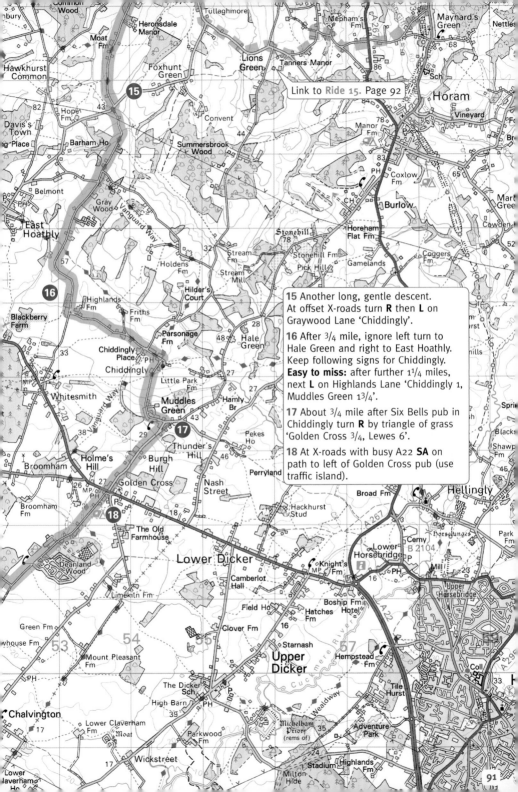

Link to **Ride 15**. Page 92

15 Another long, gentle descent. At offset X-roads turn **R** then **L** on Graywood Lane 'Chiddingly'.

16 After 3/4 mile, ignore left turn to Hale Green and right to East Hoathly. Keep following signs for Chiddingly. **Easy to miss:** after further 1¼ miles, next **L** on Highlands Lane 'Chiddingly 1, Muddles Green 1¾'.

17 About 3/4 mile after Six Bells pub in Chiddingly turn **R** by triangle of grass 'Golden Cross 3/4, Lewes 6'.

18 At X-roads with busy A22 **SA** on path to left of Golden Cross pub (use traffic island).

The Cuckoo Trail & the Sussex Weald from Heathfield

The ride starts by dropping gently south from Heathfield on the Cuckoo Trail, the most popular railway path in the South East of England, running for 11 miles down to Polegate, just to the north of Eastbourne. It is justifiably popular, with some lovely wooded sections, many sculptures, information boards and excellent views towards the South Downs. This ride leaves the Cuckoo Trail on the southern edge of Hailsham, crossing the pancake-flat Pevensey Levels on a series of quiet lanes through this distinctive geographical area. You may wish to divert off the route to visit Pevensey Castle, first a Roman fort and then a mighty Norman fortress with walls 12ft thick. After a gentle descent on the Cuckoo Trail and the flat ride across the Levels you will need to change gear to cope with the series of climbs that face you as you head north crossing many valleys formed by small streams draining south towards the Pevensey Levels or east towards Romney Marsh. The highpoint of the ride is reached at Brightling, marked by an obelisk put up by 'Mad Jack' Fuller, an eccentric MP from the 19th century. He is buried in the churchyard under a 60ft pyramid. Legend has it that he sits in a top hat and tails holding a bottle of claret. The steepest, though not the longest challenge, comes after crossing the River Dudwell as you climb up to Burwash Common. Wiggle your way through the delightful valley of the River Rother then gird your loins for the final climb up to Broad Oak, dropping from here back down to the start.

Overview

On-road ● 35 miles / 56 kilometres ● Moderate / Strenuous

Start & Parking
Cuckoo Trail car park on Station Road in Heathfield - follow signs. Heathfield is north of Eastbourne

Busy roads
About ½ mile on A265 east of Burwash Common **17**

Off-road sections
The traffic-free Cuckoo Trail is all tarmac **1** to **6**

Terrain
After a long, gentle descent down the Cuckoo Trail and a flat section across the Pevensey Levels the rest of the ride is hilly with several climbs of 100-200ft (30-60m) and four longer ones

Nearest railway
Polegate or Stonegate

Refreshments
Heathfield
Lots of choice

Hailsham
Lots of choice

A271 south of Gingers Green
Catkins Tea Room in garden centre
T: 01323 831857

Bodle Street Green
White Horse Inn
T: 01323 833243

Wood's Corner (Dallington)
Swan Inn
T: 01424 838242

Burwash Weald
Wheel Inn
T: 01435 882758

Map pages

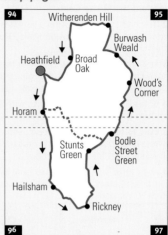

Other rides nearby

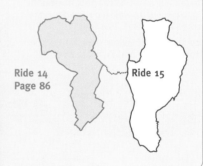

Ride 14
Page 86

Ride 15

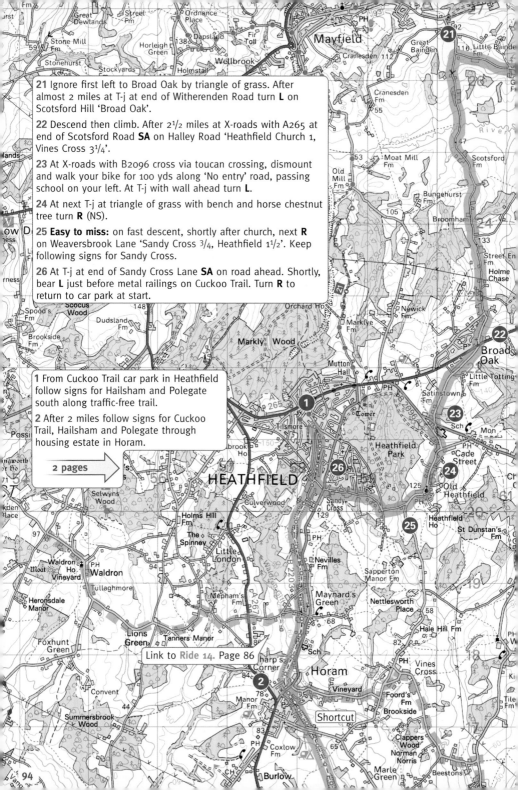

21 Ignore first left to Broad Oak by triangle of grass. After almost 2 miles at T-j at end of Witherenden Road turn **L** on Scotsford Hill 'Broad Oak'.

22 Descend then climb. After 2¹/₂ miles at X-roads with A265 at end of Scotsford Road **SA** on Halley Road 'Heathfield Church 1, Vines Cross 3¹/₄'.

23 At X-roads with B2096 cross via toucan crossing, dismount and walk your bike for 100 yds along 'No entry' road, passing school on your left. At T-j with wall ahead turn **L**.

24 At next T-j at triangle of grass with bench and horse chestnut tree turn **R** (NS).

25 **Easy to miss:** on fast descent, shortly after church, next **R** on Weaversbrook Lane 'Sandy Cross ³/₄, Heathfield 1¹/₂'. Keep following signs for Sandy Cross.

26 At T-j at end of Sandy Cross Lane **SA** on road ahead. Shortly, bear **L** just before metal railings on Cuckoo Trail. Turn **R** to return to car park at start.

1 From Cuckoo Trail car park in Heathfield follow signs for Hailsham and Polegate south along traffic-free trail.

2 After 2 miles follow signs for Cuckoo Trail, Hailsham and Polegate through housing estate in Horam.

2 pages ➡

Link to Ride 14. Page 86

Shortcut

94

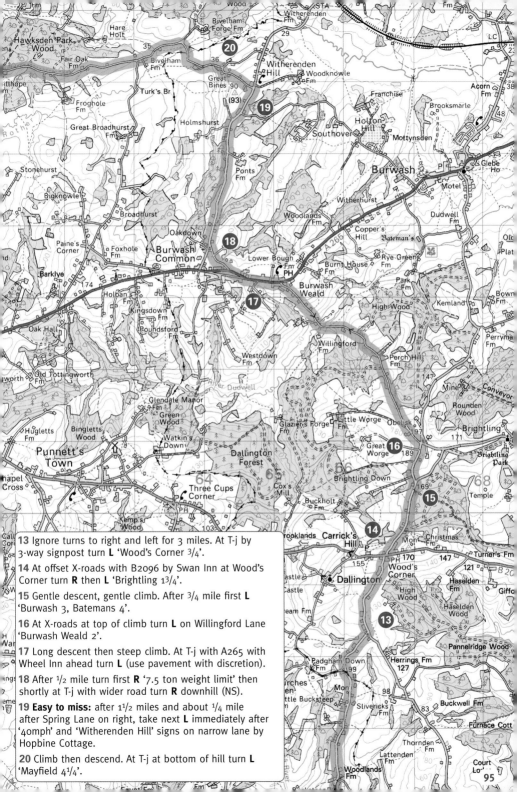

13 Ignore turns to right and left for 3 miles. At T-j by 3-way signpost turn **L** 'Wood's Corner 3/4'.

14 At offset X-roads with B2096 by Swan Inn at Wood's Corner turn **R** then **L** 'Brightling 1¾'.

15 Gentle descent, gentle climb. After 3/4 mile first **L** 'Burwash 3, Batemans 4'.

16 At X-roads at top of climb turn **L** on Willingford Lane 'Burwash Weald 2'.

17 Long descent then steep climb. At T-j with A265 with Wheel Inn ahead turn **L** (use pavement with discretion).

18 After 1/2 mile turn first **R** '7.5 ton weight limit' then shortly at T-j with wider road turn **R** downhill (NS).

19 **Easy to miss:** after 1½ miles and about ¼ mile after Spring Lane on right, take next **L** immediately after '40mph' and 'Witherenden Hill' signs on narrow lane by Hopbine Cottage.

20 Climb then descend. At T-j at bottom of hill turn **L** 'Mayfield 4¼'.

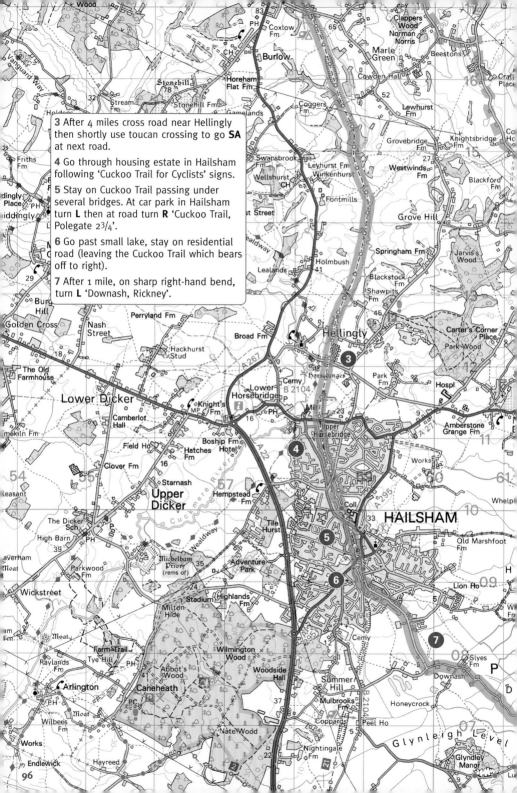

3 After 4 miles cross road near Hellingly then shortly use toucan crossing to go **SA** at next road.

4 Go through housing estate in Hailsham following 'Cuckoo Trail for Cyclists' signs.

5 Stay on Cuckoo Trail passing under several bridges. At car park in Hailsham turn **L** then at road turn **R** 'Cuckoo Trail, Polegate 2¾'.

6 Go past small lake, stay on residential road (leaving the Cuckoo Trail which bears off to right).

7 After 1 mile, on sharp right-hand bend, turn **L** 'Downash, Rickney'.

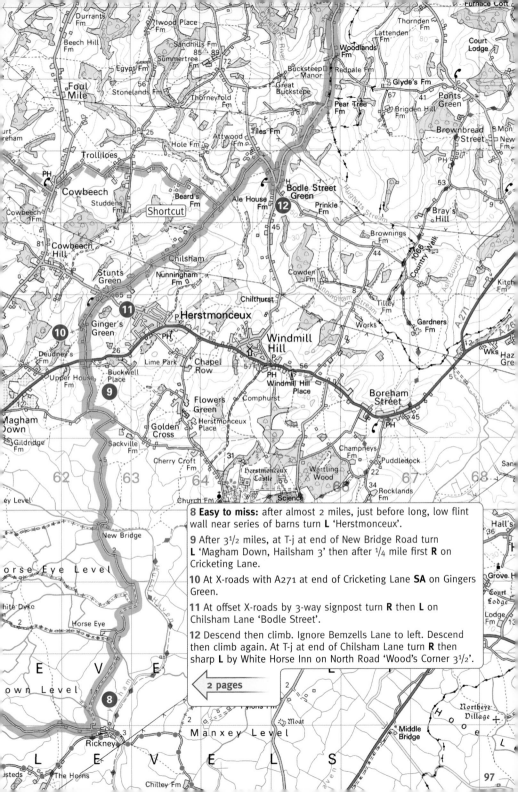

8 Easy to miss: after almost 2 miles, just before long, low flint wall near series of barns turn **L** 'Herstmonceux'.

9 After 3½ miles, at T-j at end of New Bridge Road turn **L** 'Magham Down, Hailsham 3' then after ¼ mile first **R** on Cricketing Lane.

10 At X-roads with A271 at end of Cricketing Lane **SA** on Gingers Green.

11 At offset X-roads by 3-way signpost turn **R** then **L** on Chilsham Lane 'Bodle Street'.

12 Descend then climb. Ignore Bemzells Lane to left. Descend then climb again. At T-j at end of Chilsham Lane turn **R** then sharp **L** by White Horse Inn on North Road 'Wood's Corner 3½'.

← **2 pages**

Shere, Winterfold Wood & Pitch Hill

Lying at the base of the North Downs escarpment, Shere forms a good base for exploring the byways and bridleways that radiate in all directions. You could easily amalgamate this ride with Ride 2 for a full day out. Head south on sandy tracks that climb steadily to over 700ft (210m) in Winterfold Wood. On more than one occasion the gauntlet is thrown down: can you manage the climb without a dab? There are steps, there are roots and sometimes the ground is washed out by rain,

so don't take anything for granted. After the long climb there is a short descent, at first pretty rough and narrow before a second, much easier climb, back up onto Pitch Hill. The descent starts off

gently but provides a couple of challenges, especially where the track narrows and becomes overgrown. With regard to other tracks in the area, those lying to the north of the A25 come with a health warning as the area is used by recreational 4x4 vehicles and many of the wider tracks are deep muddy ruts.

NB It is worth stressing that all off-road rides in the North Downs are better second and third time round: there are so many instructions linking the lanes and tracks that the first time is largely spent working out where to go. Once these are familiar you can enjoy the ride much more.

Overview
Off-road ● 11 miles / 18 kilometres ● Moderate / Strenuous

Start
Shere, just off the A25 between Guildford and Dorking

Parking
'Hidden' free car park in Shere. From the junction of Middle Street and Upper Street in Shere turn left towards Albury then immediately right by a '30mph' sign onto lane / track just before The Manor House. The car park is on the right

Busy roads
None

Terrain
The ride climbs south through the mixed woodland of Winterfold Wood, drops briefly then climbs again as you turn back northwards. Two main climbs:

● 425ft (130m) from Shere to the highpoint in Winterfold Wood **1** to **7**

● 265ft (80m) from the lowpoint after descending from Winterfold Wood back up to Pitch Hill **8** to **9**

Nearest railway
Gomshall

Refreshments
Shere
Prince of Wales PH
T: 01483 202313
White Horse Inn
T: 01483 202518
Lucky Duck Tearoom
T: 01483 202445

Pitch Hill (Ewhurst)
Windmill PH
T: 01483 277566

Peaslake
Hurtwood Inn
T: 01306 730851
Peaslake Village Stores
(hot drinks and snacks)

Other rides nearby

Ride 1

Ride 2
Page 102

For other rides in the area see *South East Mountain Biking – North & South Downs* by Nick Cotton

Map pages

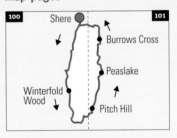

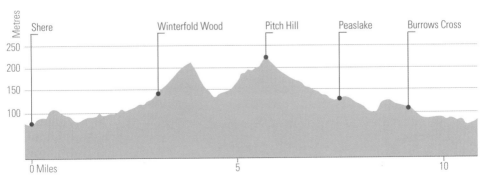

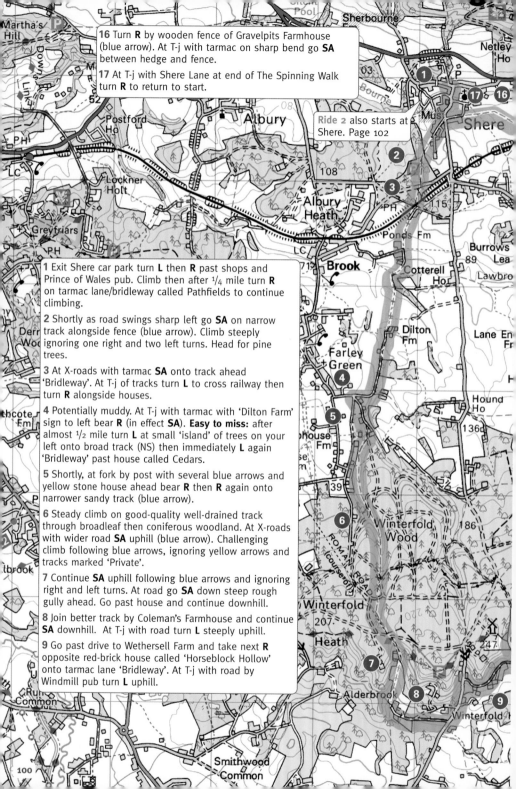

16 Turn **R** by wooden fence of Gravelpits Farmhouse (blue arrow). At T-j with tarmac on sharp bend go **SA** between hedge and fence.

17 At T-j with Shere Lane at end of The Spinning Walk turn **R** to return to start.

Ride 2 also starts at Shere. Page 102

1 Exit Shere car park turn **L** then **R** past shops and Prince of Wales pub. Climb then after ¼ mile turn **R** on tarmac lane/bridleway called Pathfields to continue climbing.

2 Shortly as road swings sharp left go **SA** on narrow track alongside fence (blue arrow). Climb steeply ignoring one right and two left turns. Head for pine trees.

3 At X-roads with tarmac **SA** onto track ahead 'Bridleway'. At T-j of tracks turn **L** to cross railway then turn **R** alongside houses.

4 Potentially muddy. At T-j with tarmac with 'Dilton Farm' sign to left bear **R** (in effect **SA**). **Easy to miss:** after almost ½ mile turn **L** at small 'island' of trees on your left onto broad track (NS) then immediately **L** again 'Bridleway' past house called Cedars.

5 Shortly, at fork by post with several blue arrows and yellow stone house ahead bear **R** then **R** again onto narrower sandy track (blue arrow).

6 Steady climb on good-quality well-drained track through broadleaf then coniferous woodland. At X-roads with wider road **SA** uphill (blue arrow). Challenging climb following blue arrows, ignoring yellow arrows and tracks marked 'Private'.

7 Continue **SA** uphill following blue arrows and ignoring right and left turns. At road go **SA** down steep rough gully ahead. Go past house and continue downhill.

8 Join better track by Coleman's Farmhouse and continue **SA** downhill. At T-j with road turn **L** steeply uphill.

9 Go past drive to Wethersell Farm and take next **R** opposite red-brick house called 'Horseblock Hollow' onto tarmac lane 'Bridleway'. At T-j with road by Windmill pub turn **L** uphill.

10 Shortly take first **R** through (open) double metal gates then turn **L** down through Hurtwood Control car park onto wide, sandy path. At fork after 1/4 mile bear **L** on lower path.

11 Fine easy descent. Go through car park and at T-j with road turn **R** then first **L** immediately after Hurtwood Inn onto Pond Lane. Ignore Burchetts Hollow then take next **R** on Jesses Lane.

12 At T-j at end of Jesses Lane turn **L**. After 100 yds first **R** on Birches Lane then immediately **R** again by wooden post onto woodland track 'Bridleway'. At fork after 150 yds bear **L** along edge of woodland, keeping field to your right.

13 At T-j of tracks by signpost with footpath/yellow arrow to left, turn **R**. May be overgrown and / or muddy.

14 At road bear **R** (in effect **SA**) by houses. Go under railway bridge then at T-j turn **L** onto High View.

15 On left-hand bend by triangle of grass and wooden bus shelter take first road **R** 'Guildford' then go **SA** onto Gravelpits Lane 'Bridleway'.

Leith Hill, highest point in South East England

Leith Hill is the highest point in South East England and, as it is surrounded by fine bridleways and byways radiating out to the north and west, it is something of a mecca for mountain biking. There is also one of the area's few waymarked singletrack forestry trails, known as 'Summer Lightning'. For the most relevant information about this it is best to use Internet search engines: you will find out the most up-to-date state of the trail and about other routes in the area. The ride starts from the attractive village of Shere

where there are several eating places to look forward to on your return. The ride heads east along the valley on predominantly broad sandy tracks as far as the edge of Westcott, before turning south and climbing almost 700ft (210m) with some testing challenges along the way. Leith Hill Tower is open at the weekends and there are some stupendous views on fine, clear days. This is a popular area for all sorts of users so please show consideration to walkers in the vicinity of the tower as you descend to the road. A second climb takes you up towards Holmbury

Hill and the longer, rougher descent back down towards Abinger. There is one stretch where there seem to be more badgers than bikers. The outward route is briefly rejoined to take you back to Shere.

Overview
Off-road ● **17 miles / 27 kilometres** ● **Strenuous**

Start
Shere, just off the A25 between Guildford and Dorking

Parking
'Hidden' free car park in Shere. From the junction of Middle Street and Upper Street in Shere turn left towards Albury then immediately right by a '30mph' sign on lane / track just before The Manor House. The car park is on the right

Busy roads
The A25 is used for ¼ mile west of Abinger Hammer

Terrain
Gentle gradients along the valley as far as Westcott. Two major climbs follow:

● A sustained 695ft (211m) climb to the top of Leith Hill **12** to **16**

● Steep 395ft (120m) climb on Holmbury Hill **18** to **19**

Nearest railway
Gomshall

Refreshments
Shere
Prince of Wales
T: 01483 202313
White Horse Inn
T: 01483 202518
Lucky Duck Tearoom
T: 01483 202445

Abinger Hammer
Abinger Arms
T: 01306 730145

Coldharbour
Plough Inn
T: 01306 711793

Leith Hill Tower
Café at weekends

Other rides nearby

Ride 1
Page 98

For other rides in the area see *South East Mountain Biking – North & South Downs* by Nick Cotton

Map pages

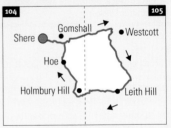

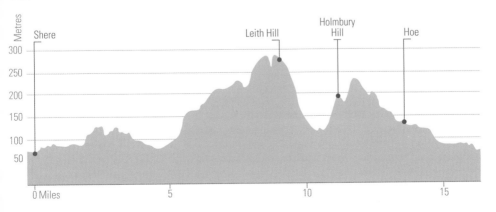

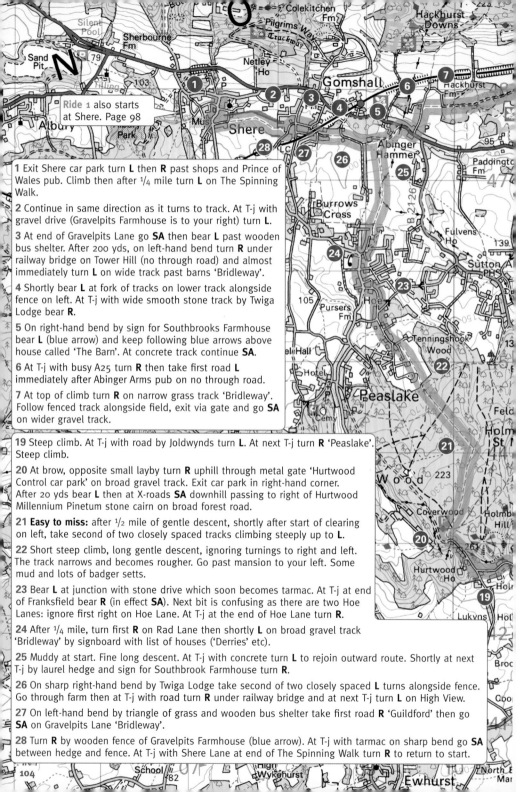

1 Exit Shere car park turn **L** then **R** past shops and Prince of Wales pub. Climb then after ¼ mile turn **L** on The Spinning Walk.

2 Continue in same direction as it turns to track. At T-j with gravel drive (Gravelpits Farmhouse is to your right) turn **L**.

3 At end of Gravelpits Lane go **SA** then bear **L** past wooden bus shelter. After 200 yds, on left-hand bend turn **R** under railway bridge on Tower Hill (no through road) and almost immediately turn **L** on wide track past barns 'Bridleway'.

4 Shortly bear **L** at fork of tracks on lower track alongside fence on left. At T-j with wide smooth stone track by Twiga Lodge bear **R**.

5 On right-hand bend by sign for Southbrooks Farmhouse bear **L** (blue arrow) and keep following blue arrows above house called 'The Barn'. At concrete track continue **SA**.

6 At T-j with busy A25 turn **R** then take first road **L** immediately after Abinger Arms pub on no through road.

7 At top of climb turn **R** on narrow grass track 'Bridleway'. Follow fenced track alongside field, exit via gate and go **SA** on wider gravel track.

19 Steep climb. At T-j with road by Joldwynds turn **L**. At next T-j turn **R** 'Peaslake'. Steep climb.

20 At brow, opposite small layby turn **R** uphill through metal gate 'Hurtwood Control car park' on broad gravel track. Exit car park in right-hand corner. After 20 yds bear **L** then at X-roads **SA** downhill passing to right of Hurtwood Millennium Pinetum stone cairn on broad forest road.

21 Easy to miss: after ½ mile of gentle descent, shortly after start of clearing on left, take second of two closely spaced tracks climbing steeply up to **L**.

22 Short steep climb, long gentle descent, ignoring turnings to right and left. The track narrows and becomes rougher. Go past mansion to your left. Some mud and lots of badger setts.

23 Bear **L** at junction with stone drive which soon becomes tarmac. At T-j at end of Franksfield bear **R** (in effect **SA**). Next bit is confusing as there are two Hoe Lanes: ignore first right on Hoe Lane. At T-j at the end of Hoe Lane turn **R**.

24 After ¼ mile, turn first **R** on Rad Lane then shortly **L** on broad gravel track 'Bridleway' by signboard with list of houses ('Derries' etc).

25 Muddy at start. Fine long descent. At T-j with concrete turn **L** to rejoin outward route. Shortly at next T-j by laurel hedge and sign for Southbrook Farmhouse turn **R**.

26 On sharp right-hand bend by Twiga Lodge take second of two closely spaced **L** turns alongside fence. Go through farm then at T-j with road turn **R** under railway bridge and at next T-j turn **L** on High View.

27 On left-hand bend by triangle of grass and wooden bus shelter take first road **R** 'Guildford' then go **SA** on Gravelpits Lane 'Bridleway'.

28 Turn **R** by wooden fence of Gravelpits Farmhouse (blue arrow). At T-j with tarmac on sharp bend go **SA** between hedge and fence. At T-j with Shere Lane at end of The Spinning Walk turn **R** to return to start.

Ride 1 also starts at Shere. Page 98

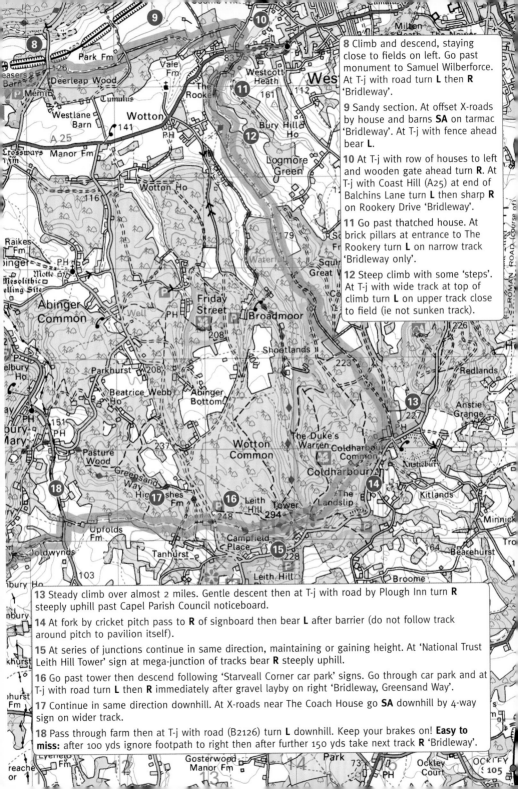

8 Climb and descend, staying close to fields on left. Go past monument to Samuel Wilberforce. At T-j with road turn **L** then **R** 'Bridleway'.

9 Sandy section. At offset X-roads by house and barns **SA** on tarmac 'Bridleway'. At T-j with fence ahead bear **L**.

10 At T-j with row of houses to left and wooden gate ahead turn **R**. At T-j with Coast Hill (A25) at end of Balchins Lane turn **L** then sharp **R** on Rookery Drive 'Bridleway'.

11 Go past thatched house. At brick pillars at entrance to The Rookery turn **L** on narrow track 'Bridleway only'.

12 Steep climb with some 'steps'. At T-j with wide track at top of climb turn **L** on upper track close to field (ie not sunken track).

13 Steady climb over almost 2 miles. Gentle descent then at T-j with road by Plough Inn turn **R** steeply uphill past Capel Parish Council noticeboard.

14 At fork by cricket pitch pass to **R** of signboard then bear **L** after barrier (do not follow track around pitch to pavilion itself).

15 At series of junctions continue in same direction, maintaining or gaining height. At 'National Trust Leith Hill Tower' sign at mega-junction of tracks bear **R** steeply uphill.

16 Go past tower then descend following 'Starveall Corner car park' signs. Go through car park and at T-j with road turn **L** then **R** immediately after gravel layby on right 'Bridleway, Greensand Way'.

17 Continue in same direction downhill. At X-roads near The Coach House go **SA** downhill by 4-way sign on wider track.

18 Pass through farm then at T-j with road (B2126) turn **L** downhill. Keep your brakes on! **Easy to miss:** after 100 yds ignore footpath to right then after further 150 yds take next track **R** 'Bridleway'.

Godstone, Oxted & the North Downs

Putting together mountain bike routes in the North Downs involves lots of short sections of track connected to short sections of tarmac – this is unavoidable as there are few long, unbroken sections of bridleway / byway in the area. This can present route-finding challenges first time round, but the rides tend to get better as you do them a second and third time and come to know where to go at each junction, or where to sneak off down that narrow hidden track. This ride is an exploration of the sand and chalk tracks between Oxted and Caterham with a couple of odd twists: shortly after leaving Godstone there is a gate that mysteriously opens by itself, then later, as you pass by Barrow Green Court just before the bridge over the M25, every post seems to have a security camera on it trained on anyone walking, riding or cycling along the perimeter. Spooky! A short tarmac warm-up south from Godstone takes you to the start of the first off-road section, as ever in these parts, a series of short linking stretches of track. Bypass Oxted and climb steeply after crossing the M25. How far can you climb without a dab? Enjoy the views from high up on the North Downs before dropping fast on good woodland tracks on Gravelly Hill and around the sand pit. Fancy a beer in Bletchingley? The last off-road section wanders through woods and past paddocks before a fast tarmac descent to Godstone.

Overview

Off-road ● 15 miles / 24 kilometres ● Moderate

Start
Godstone, east of Reigate
(south of M25, junction 6)

Parking
By the pond and around the
green near the White Hart pub

Busy roads
None

Terrain
The southern half of the ride
undulates between 295ft
(90m) and 425ft (130m).
There is one major climb

● 460ft (140m) from Oxted
north of the M25 to the top of
the North Downs escarpment
on Tandridge Hill

Nearest railway
Oxted

Refreshments
Godstone
Lots of choice

Oxted
Lots of choice

Bletchingley
Whyte Hart PH
T: 01883 743231
Prince Albert PH
T: 01883 743257

Other rides nearby
For other rides in the area see
*South East Mountain Biking –
North & South Downs* by Nick
Cotton

Map pages

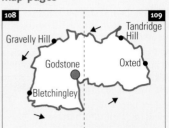

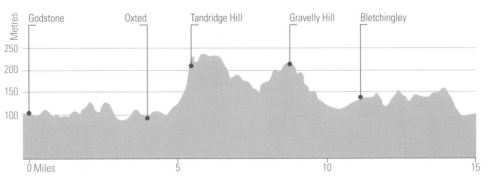

12 Track turns to concrete then tarmac. Follow road **L** downhill past Spaceworks factory then, **easy to miss**, shortly, on left-hand bend on descent, turn **R** sharply back on yourself uphill on wide gravel track 'National Cycle Network Route 21 (NCN 21), Bridleway'.

13 At T-j with A22 dual carriageway turn **L** on cyclepath, cross bridge then bear **L** steeply uphill on lane. Immediately after Downs Residential Site turn **L** on track by metal bollards (stone 'Bridleway' marker).

14 At T-j with better track bear **R** gently uphill 'North Downs Way' (blue arrow). At T-j with road by Caterham Viewpoint turn **L** then shortly bear **L** 'NCN 21, North Downs Way' (blue arrow).

15 At fork bear **L** to continue downhill 'NCN 21' (North Downs Way footpath is to your right) then shortly at X-roads of tracks bear **R** 'NCN 21' (blue arrow).

16 Keep following NCN 21 signs, eventually turning **L*** at X-roads of tracks with small rickety shed in field on left. Go under M25. At T-j with road turn **L** and follow round right-hand bend.

***If you hit tarmac and see drive on left to White Hill House you have come 100 yds too far. Retrace.**

17 At X-roads with busy A25 in Bletchingley go **SA** on Outwood Lane. After ¹/₄ mile, at end of houses turn **L** by 50mph speed signs then immediately **L** again 'Bridleway'.

18 Go past pond then just after top of climb turn **R** downhill on narrow track between two concrete posts towards field. At first rough. Continue **SA** downhill on narrow track at X-roads of tracks with locked metal gate to right. Soon join fine, level track.

19 At T-j with road bear **L** uphill then shortly bear **R** 'Bridleway' on wide gravel track. At road turn **L** uphill for 200 yds then keep an eye out for track to **R** 'Bridleway'.

20 At T-j with road turn **L**. Climb then descend. At T-j with old A22 turn **L** to return to Godstone.

1 With back to White Hart pub in Godstone (by pond) turn **L** on B2236 towards East Grinstead. At end of houses on left, first **L** '6ft 6ins width limit'.

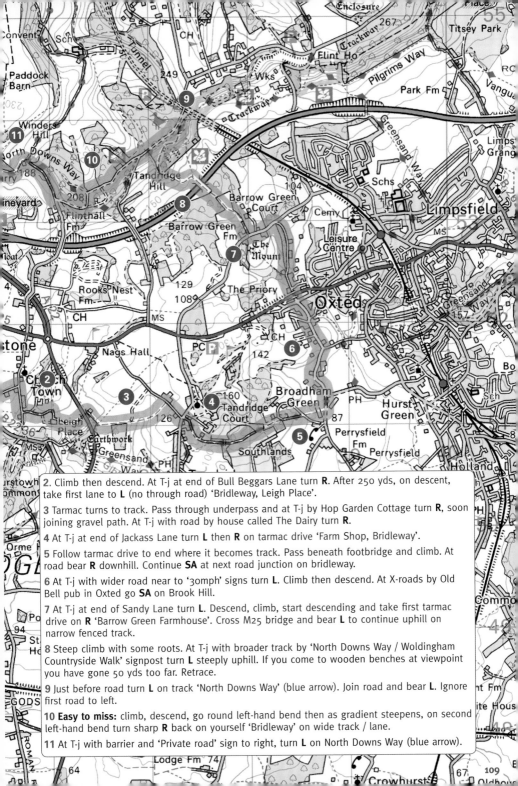

2. Climb then descend. At T-j at end of Bull Beggars Lane turn **R**. After 250 yds, on descent, take first lane to **L** (no through road) 'Bridleway, Leigh Place'.

3 Tarmac turns to track. Pass through underpass and at T-j by Hop Garden Cottage turn **R**, soon joining gravel path. At T-j with road by house called The Dairy turn **R**.

4 At T-j at end of Jackass Lane turn **L** then **R** on tarmac drive 'Farm Shop, Bridleway'.

5 Follow tarmac drive to end where it becomes track. Pass beneath footbridge and climb. At road bear **R** downhill. Continue **SA** at next road junction on bridleway.

6 At T-j with wider road near to '30mph' signs turn **L**. Climb then descend. At X-roads by Old Bell pub in Oxted go **SA** on Brook Hill.

7 At T-j at end of Sandy Lane turn **L**. Descend, climb, start descending and take first tarmac drive on **R** 'Barrow Green Farmhouse'. Cross M25 bridge and bear **L** to continue uphill on narrow fenced track.

8 Steep climb with some roots. At T-j with broader track by 'North Downs Way / Woldingham Countryside Walk' signpost turn **L** steeply uphill. If you come to wooden benches at viewpoint you have gone 50 yds too far. Retrace.

9 Just before road turn **L** on track 'North Downs Way' (blue arrow). Join road and bear **L**. Ignore first road to left.

10 Easy to miss: climb, descend, go round left-hand bend then as gradient steepens, on second left-hand bend turn sharp **R** back on yourself 'Bridleway' on wide track / lane.

11 At T-j with barrier and 'Private road' sign to right, turn **L** on North Downs Way (blue arrow).

South Downs Way – Bignor Hill & Graffham Down

A car park favoured by motorbikers by a roundabout at the junction of two busy A roads seems an unlikely place to start a mountain bike ride, but within a matter of seconds you slip away on forest tracks, leaving behind the noise and fumes, soon joining the South Downs Way as it climbs to the west up over Bignor Hill. Keep an eye out for the tall sign with Latin names indicating the area's connection with the Romans: in this case the old Roman Road of Stane Street, which crossed Bignor Hill on its way from Chichester to London. Head for the masts on Glatting Beacon, cruise along the ridge then prepare yourself for the fast chalk descent down to the A285 (slippery when wet!). The next climb is the toughest of the day, at first using wide chalk tracks then crossing two fields that get very sticky after winter rains. Another level section follows through woodland before a fabulous long descent down to the road near East Dean (your only chance of refreshment). Lanes and broad forest tracks lead all the way back to the start. If the wide tracks are covered in puddles, always keep an eye out for singletrack alternatives threading their way through the trees to the left or the right of the main track. A quick glance at a map will show you that all the way west to the A3 the area is criss-crossed with bridleways, so this is just one of dozens of routes available nearby.

Overview

Off-road ● 15 miles / 24 kilometres ● Moderate / Strenuous

Start & Parking
Free car park at roundabout at junction of A29, A284 and B2139 north of Arundel

Busy roads
None

Terrain
The ride is largely along the ridge of the South Downs escarpment or just to the south of it with several 100-200ft (30-60m) climbs and three longer ones:

● 425ft (130m) from the start to Glatting Beacon (the climb comes in three separate sections) **1** to **6**

● 415ft (126m) from crossing the A285 up on Littleton Down **8**

● 270ft (83m) south from the Forestry Commission car park at Droke to the road at Selhurst Park **12**

Nearest railway
Amberley

Refreshments
Café in car park at the start

East Dean
Star & Garter PH
T: 01243 811318

Shortcut
There are several shortcut options in the Bignor Hill, Glatting Beacon area from the north side of the route to the south side

Other rides nearby

Ride 4

**Ride 5
Page 114**

For other rides in the area see *South East Mountain Biking – North & South Downs* by Nick Cotton

Map pages

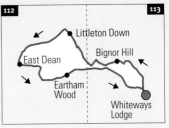

112   113

Littleton Down

Bignor Hill

East Dean

Eartham Wood

Whiteways Lodge

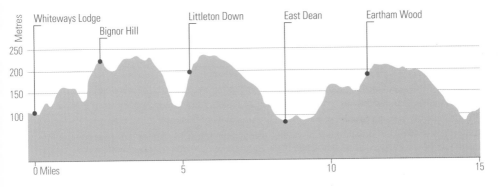

Whiteways Lodge

Bignor Hill

Littleton Down

East Dean

Eartham Wood

Metres

250

200

150

100

0 Miles   5   10   15

7 At X-roads with the A285 at bottom of fine descent turn **R** then **L** on similar track.

8 Climb, passing through two large fields (the second field may have been ploughed with a rough path running diagonally across it). Enter woodland.

9 At exit of woodland at X-roads of tracks by large 'Tegleaze' post turn **L** 'East Dean, Public Right of Way' (red arrow). After 200 yds at fork bear **R** on track running between fence and edge of woodland.

10 At major forest road junction continue **SA** downhill on track running as straight as an arrow.

11 Long descent through woodland on fine track. At T-j with road with red-brick semi-detached house ahead turn **L**.

12 After 1 mile on sharp left-hand bend by 'Forestry Commission Droke' signboard turn **R** to go past right-hand barrier and climb steadily on broad stone track. At T-j with road turn **L** (NS).

13 At junction with A285 go **SA** on left-hand of two tracks ahead 'Bridleway'.

14 Long climb on broad woodland track. If muddy, use parallel tracks to right or left. Emerge from forest and continue **SA** on obvious stone and grass track. At fork after 300 yds by 3-way bridleway signpost bear **R** on lower, broader track.

1 Exit top end of car park towards wood via wide red metal gate and (**easy to miss**) keep an eye out for first narrow stone track uphill to **R** by post with blue arrow.

2 Soon, at T-j turn **L** following field edge uphill and round to **R** (may be overgrown). Steady climb. At T-j with South Downs Way bear **L** uphill on broader track.

3 Climb, flat section, downhill. After 1 mile at junction of tracks immediately beyond metal barns turn **L** to continue on South Downs Way.

4 At T-j at top of steep climb turn **R** 'South Downs Way' to continue more gently uphill.

5 At car park at top, pass to **R** of tall wooden signpost with Roman names and 'No cars' sign on broad chalk and flint track towards masts.

6 At fork on exit from woodland containing masts turn **L**. Shortly at next track junction by a 5-way post and 'National Trust Slindon Estate' sign turn sharp **R** 'South Downs Way'.

Link to **Ride 5**. Page 114

15 At next fork by 3-way signpost with mast up to your left continue SA 'Bridleway. Gumber Bothy 1600 metres'. At major track junction by 4-way signpost **SA** gently uphill.

16 After 1/3 mile at X-roads of tracks at end of field on right and shortly after wooden bench to left, go **SA** (blue arrow).

17 After almost 2 miles at X-roads at bottom of long easy descent **SA** (blue arrow) to return to car park at start.

Amberley & Kithurst Hill

Amberley Station and Amberley are two separate settlements connected by the B2139, a fast and busy road, hence the starting point for this ride on a minor lane north of the station. Climb steadily on tarmac then off-road before discovering a secret hidden dry valley full of cowslips in the summer. Can you make it up the other side? You will need strength, stamina and dry conditions. Drop back down into the Arun Valley on a series of broad chalk and flint tracks. Burpham's pub is definitely an upmarket gastropub rather than a centre for mountain bikers but there are tables outside if you fancy a break. The southern section is the most prone to mud,

but the wide tracks through woodland often have parallel singletracks that offer drier alternatives. The steady climb from Lee Farm leads up to the South Downs ridge and a long, splendid, easy section with magnificent views down into the Sussex Weald. In its entirety the 100-mile South Downs Way from Winchester to Eastbourne makes a fantastic linear mountain bike ride that can be done over

a weekend. To ride it in just two days you must get the planning right: do it after a few hot, dry days sometime between May and early October (so that the tracks are dry and fast, not wet and sticky) and organise logistics so that you are carrying an absolute minimum i.e. dump stuff at your overnight stop before starting the ride so the bikes perform like mountain bikes and not pack horses.

Overview

Off-road ● 16 miles / 26 kilometres ● Moderate / Strenuous

Start & Parking

The village of Amberley Station, on the B2139 north of Littlehampton and Arundel. The main car park in Amberley by the museum / train station is ONLY for visitors to the museum. Continue east on the B2139 under the railway bridge, then after 1/4 mile turn right on the lane called High Titten and park here

Busy roads

None if you avoid the B2139 past Amberley Station

Terrain

The River Arun is one of the few rivers that cut through the South Downs. The river is tidal in Amberley and the land rises steeply up to almost 700ft (210m). There are several short steep climbs (mainly in the first half of the ride) and two longer ones:

● 270ft (82m) on tarmac then track right from the start ❶ to ❷

● 375ft (115m) from Lee Farm to the South Downs Way on Kithurst Hill ⑬ to ⑭

Nearest railway

Amberley

Refreshments

Amberley
Lots of choice

Burpham
George & Dragon PH
T: 01903 883131

Other rides nearby

Ride 4
Page 110

Ride 5

Map pages

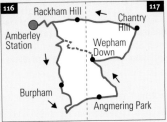

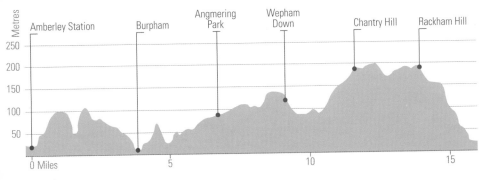

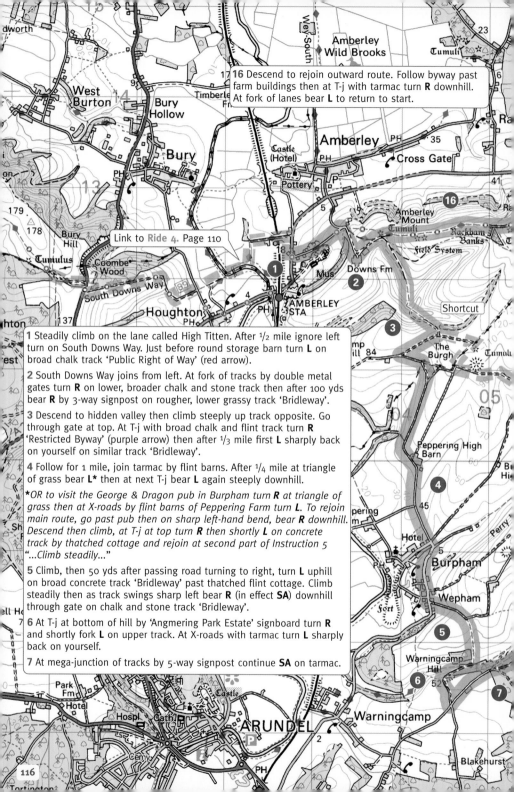

16 Descend to rejoin outward route. Follow byway past farm buildings then at T-j with tarmac turn **R** downhill. At fork of lanes bear **L** to return to start.

Link to **Ride 4**. Page 110

Shortcut

1 Steadily climb on the lane called High Titten. After ½ mile ignore left turn on South Downs Way. Just before round storage barn turn **L** on broad chalk track 'Public Right of Way' (red arrow).

2 South Downs Way joins from left. At fork of tracks by double metal gates turn **R** on lower, broader chalk and stone track then after 100 yds bear **R** by 3-way signpost on rougher, lower grassy track 'Bridleway'.

3 Descend to hidden valley then climb steeply up track opposite. Go through gate at top. At T-j with broad chalk and flint track turn **R** 'Restricted Byway' (purple arrow) then after ⅓ mile first **L** sharply back on yourself on similar track 'Bridleway'.

4 Follow for 1 mile, join tarmac by flint barns. After ¼ mile at triangle of grass bear **L*** then at next T-j bear **L** again steeply downhill.

****OR** to visit the George & Dragon pub in Burpham turn **R** at triangle of grass then at X-roads by flint barns of Peppering Farm turn **L**. To rejoin main route, go past pub then on sharp left-hand bend, bear **R** downhill. Descend then climb, at T-j at top turn **R** then shortly **L** on concrete track by thatched cottage and rejoin at second part of Instruction 5 "...Climb steadily..."*

5 Climb, then 50 yds after passing road turning to right, turn **L** uphill on broad concrete track 'Bridleway' past thatched flint cottage. Climb steadily then as track swings sharp left bear **R** (in effect **SA**) downhill through gate on chalk and stone track 'Bridleway'.

6 At T-j at bottom of hill by 'Angmering Park Estate' signboard turn **R** and shortly fork **L** on upper track. At X-roads with tarmac turn **L** sharply back on yourself.

7 At mega-junction of tracks by 5-way signpost continue **SA** on tarmac.

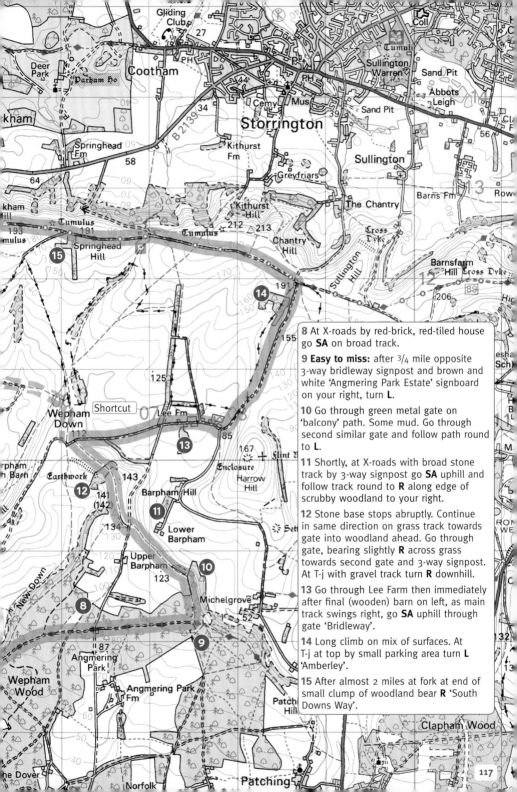

8 At X-roads by red-brick, red-tiled house go **SA** on broad track.

9 **Easy to miss:** after ³/₄ mile opposite 3-way bridleway signpost and brown and white 'Angmering Park Estate' signboard on your right, turn **L**.

10 Go through green metal gate on 'balcony' path. Some mud. Go through second similar gate and follow path round to **L**.

11 Shortly, at X-roads with broad stone track by 3-way signpost go **SA** uphill and follow track round to **R** along edge of scrubby woodland to your right.

12 Stone base stops abruptly. Continue in same direction on grass track towards gate into woodland ahead. Go through gate, bearing slightly **R** across grass towards second gate and 3-way signpost. At T-j with gravel track turn **R** downhill.

13 Go through Lee Farm then immediately after final (wooden) barn on left, as main track swings right, go **SA** uphill through gate 'Bridleway'.

14 Long climb on mix of surfaces. At T-j at top by small parking area turn **L** 'Amberley'.

15 After almost 2 miles at fork at end of small clump of woodland bear **R** 'South Downs Way'.